A Love So Mighty

A True Story of God's Transforming Presence

Erinn J. Campton

To the Monday Night Prayer Warriors, for the tireless love you show to all.

Contents

Acknowledgements

With an outpouring of gratitude, I thank You, Heavenly Father, for giving me a story to tell. Thank You, Holy Spirit for Your ever-present guidance. Thank You Jesus, for being the foundation I stand on in prayer.

Special thanks to:

To my husband, Ty, for surrendering your talents, your time, and your efforts in supporting this book and all others that will come after it. Thank you for not letting me give up, for having faith in my sanity when I act crazy, and for being my soulmate.

Thank you to my sweet little boy; I am astonished daily by the pure and powerful love you show anyone who crosses your path. You were designed to bring joy and laughter. I am so proud of everything you do.

Mama, my editor, cheerleader, voice of reason, and biggest fan. You cannot know the impact you have on my life and the lives of your grandchildren. You have refined this work with the amazing talents God gave you. You raised me to be a person who reaches out to others in love. And because you made me write this down as it was happening, we together have a testimony that will change people's lives. Mama, we did it! And I am so pleased with our performance!

To Papa, Toni, Bennie, and the rest of my family, what a God-given treasure all of you are. No matter how people respond to this message, I know I have a cheering section and I hold your love. Please know that it is returned unconditionally.

To Debra Wilson and Beverly Nickerson for investing your time, prayer, insight, and encouragement into the release of this testimony. Thank you to the Healing Rooms team for being my heaven-given family.

To my Launch Team:

Paula Anderson, Allie Brown, Emily Brown, Kendall Buckley, Alisha Campton, Judy Campton, Staci Campton, Linda Clancy, Kathleen Cloud, Ann Donelson, Meg Fink, Adam "Vibe" Gunton, Kelly Hardison, Staci Harris, Madeline Herboldsheimer,, Lynn Ann Huizingh, Terri Jacobs, Hannah Jelinek, Jennifer Kelley, LeAnne Kelly, Kadi LaMarr, Kathleen Martinez, Brenda Miller, Corina Haley Miller, Nicole Montey, John and Mary Ann Musciano, Kathleen Munroe, Delisa Novak, Mariah Puckett, Melanie Roberts, Megan Slominski, Peggy Sowell, Dee Thye, Teri Turcotte, Kayla Whitney, Eric Williams, Shannon Williams, Norma Jean Wilson, Gloria Zebari

You are the start of something that will breathe life into many dark corners for people. You are called to begin a movement of joy and hope in your circles of influence and it is my sincere prayer that this testimony will prove to be a powerful tool for that calling. From the bottom of my heart, thank you for coming alongside me in the spreading of this message. You will be blessed for it, in the name of Jesus!

And finally, thank you reader. You are here because you know there is more than meets the eye in this life and you are hungry for it. May this testimony encourage you as you encounter God's presence.

Prologue. Send Me.

His Spirit speaks.

I will go before you and make the crooked places straight, He says. *I will break in pieces the gates of brass and cut in sunder the bars of iron.* 1

The words echo within from Someone who formed the end of this story before my first breath.

I struggle in the telling of this message and prove myself unworthy of it daily. How do I show you what God transformed in the life of Gwen? Or in my own?

One winter morning my friend decided to die, and it changed everything.

And the Lord wants me to tell them.

Lord, how do I tell them?

I fight to understand, but much remains a mystery.

Mystery is vital on the journey of belief in Jesus. We take Our Father's hand, accept a childmind, and follow Him onto stormy waters with trust in the heart and song on the lips.

What a year it's been. A year of hope and pain, growth, and loss. A year of healing.

Peering through the film of greasy child fingerprints and dog-nose smudges out my bay window to the street, I remember a time just over 12 months ago.

I see me, a different me, struggling to turn the secondhand stroller from my driveway onto the cracked sidewalk. Leroy, a baby not yet one year, gazes up at me with joy; his fluffy blonde hair ruffles like soft feathers in the morning sunlight.

"Do you hear the trash truck? I bet it's close!" My past self says.

This enthusiasm for the trash truck was new then, a byproduct of mothering a motor-minded boy. Leroy's pudgy baby finger points at the truck then up to show his mama a plane flying low.

This is it! It is about to begin! I want to wave and call to myself. *You have no idea what you are about to walk into. . .*

Part I:

Off the Chair

Divine Appointment Set
Gwendolynn Lopez with Erinn and Leroy
Campton
Monday, May 29th – Memorial Day
9:52AM
Abeja Street

I stroll Leroy through the neighborhood on a clear spring morning. His first birthday nears — soon he will change from squishy baby to a toddling whirling dervish.

Leroy reveres the trashman with his trash-grabbing truck. We hunt for a sighting of this waste-removing conqueror, pressing onward over the crumbling concrete of an old sidewalk.

Four houses pass, and we stumble upon a different kind of hero. My neighbor, soon to be friend, Gwendolynn.

She rests on her front porch in a backless wicker chair. Her hair hangs past her shoulders, a heavy-bodied rusty grey. She wears simple jeans and a flowing shirt adorned by southwestern designs. At her feet is a black mutt with soft eyes and a greying muzzle.

When she see us, she puts out a cigarette, and smiles. A smile that impacts her entire face. Joyful wrinkles crease at her temples and nose as she looks out at my child.

4

"It's a good day to take in some sun!" I call.

"Isn't it gorgeous?" Her palms rise to the spring sunlight.

I slow the stroller as I pass, "It's nice to have a day off this time of year."

Gwen shrugs, her smile melting and open palms dropping into fists. "I'm sorry to say I don't have a choice. I would rather work. I was just diagnosed with end stage kidney failure and it forced me out. All my days are a day off now. I wish I could have another day 'on'."

A death sentence. So much for casual greetings.

"I'm sorry to hear that." I stop short and study her closer. She seems too young and fit for kidney failure. Mid-50s. Petite. Clear tan skin. Aside from the smoking habit, she appears healthy. "Has anyone prayed over you to be healed?" The words pour from my mouth with an uncharacteristic boldness, but if not for this, what has God been training me for?

"Are you a Christian?" Her troubled face transforms into excitement.

I fight the cumbersome stroller up her driveway and we stand in the shade of her carport to escape the heat. "I am. The Lord calls me to pray for healing. Would you mind if I prayed over you?"

She nods with enthusiasm, then continues to share, "The sickness started last year. I felt breathless trying to climb stairs at work. Then I would get so confused — that was the weirdest thing. I worked the same darn job for a decade but all of the sudden I would just find myself staring at my computer, not knowing what to do. I remember thinking, '*What the heck! I must be getting old!*'"

Leroy interrupts her story by showing her a special rock he brought along for our journey.

She laughs and bends down to talk to him. "Ah yes, what a nice rock! What is your name? My goodness you are cute. Look how big you are!" He grins and reaches for her. Gwen takes his tiny hands in hers and croons to him while I wait for the rest of her story. She covers the side of her mouth to whisper a secret to me, "I think I have some lollipops. Can he have a lollipop yet?"

"Not yet, but you'll be the first to know when that changes." I laugh.

Leroy grips her hand. She crouches down to hold it while she continues, "When I started to swell up and itch I decided to get some blood work done. Part of me had to know, because an hour before I received the results, I told my son we needed to start praying as a family. Then we got the call, my kidneys had stopped functioning."

"I'm going to die of this. Which is okay, don't get me wrong! I know where I am going, and I look forward to what comes next. I just don't want to suffer here.

Nothing would be worse than this illness dragging on. My mom went through it for years and I don't want that to be my story."

I've learned not to accept anything other than what Scripture decrees. "Your story will be different." I tell her. "Let's turn this over to God. Your diagnosis doesn't get the final say, He does." I lay a hand on her shoulder and one on her head, we bow before God inside an old carport, praying over the noise of a neighbor mowing his lawn.

This moment our combined cry to the Lord forged an alliance, driven by the Holy Spirit, a relationship in significance beyond my comprehension.

I don't want to tell you the truth, but you deserve to know it. I didn't like Gwen at first.

In my defense, Gwen is consumed with self-pity regarding her diagnosis. Bitterness churns beneath the surface of an otherwise funny, generous, and thoughtful woman. Her contaminated worldview makes her pessimistic and an unpleasant conversationalist. Through my discomfort in her company I remind myself of her fight. This illness rises as her greatest mountain.

But this was more than just not feeling like being around someone. Something beyond my understanding repelled me from her. Every time I felt the Lord urging me to reach out, I pulled against Him. He was relentless though, and most of the time I surrendered to His request.

Over the following months, God nudged me to pause in my busyness and asked me to connect with Gwen. We went on walks and enjoyed coffee dates. Anytime I got swept up in my overwhelming list of Mom duties, He reminded me to send a word of encouragement. I wish I could say I always responded to God's urging like a saint, but often I would argue, "I enjoy my privacy and solitude," I rationalized. "Can I call her tomorrow? Can I walk a different way, so I don't pass her house?"

Once we are together, Gwen's love for Leroy rewards my obedience. My son's deep connection with Gwen converts my dislike into admiration. Their closeness grows. They greet each other with excitement and kisses. Leroy points to her house, telling me in baby language to stop for a visit.

When I took him trick-or-treating he was shy and reserved until we reached Gwen's familiar porch. The second she opened the door, Leroy ran past and into her home helping himself to everything on the coffee table. He knows where he is welcome and loved. We leave with a bag full of lollipops in our hands and Gwen's laughter in our hearts.

During our times together, I am called to try to re-direct Gwen's pessimism with reminders of God's goodness. I discover Gwen's concern over her living situation. She struggles to make mortgage payments on her meager disability checks. The cost of living in our area continues to rise.

"I need the basement finished on this house." She laments. "With a finished basement my son can move in with his family and help with bills. If this doesn't happen, I may lose my home."

And soon worse does come to worse.

A few weeks before Christmas, as I sped down the highway, my spirit again was urged to call her. Her sweet old dog passed away and she missed a mortgage payment.

"I would rather be dead than destitute." She says through tears.

"This isn't over, Gwen. There is a lot of money in the world. We just need to figure out how to apply it to your house. We can find a way to do this. I bet there are many contractors who would be willing to help with free services if they knew what you're going through! After the holidays, come over and we will create a flyer asking for these guys. We can put it up at all the churches around here."

"You really think people would help me?"

"I do. People out there want to do His work, some just don't know where to go to get it done."

Gwen takes a deep breath, her tears spent. "Okay, after the holidays."

January is the month of fresh starts and renewed mindsets. It's a relief to arrive at a routine again after the holiday madness. This morning I catch up on my laundry mountain.

I toss damp clothes into the dryer and recall a conversation from weeks ago. Something about a remodel for Gwen's basement.

The still, small voice₂ of the Holy Spirit speaks, **Text Gwen.**

Okay, Lord. I will when I finish. I pull out wet jeans.

Text Gwen right now.

The Boss has spoken.

I drop the jeans on the edge of the washer and I seek out my phone, this time without a fight. Weeks have passed since Gwen and I last spoke, I realize I miss seeing her as I send the text. *"Hey sis, wanna come over tomorrow? I started a flyer to help raise $ for the house!"*

I check my phone for an answer a few times, but the screen stays empty.

Her response finally comes the following evening. When my phone rings past 8 p.m. and I see Gwen's name, I watch it chime as I weigh the hour and the level of my exhaustion.

It is late for us, maybe I should call her back tomorrow. I grapple, then answer. "Hey girl," I keep my voice soft, so I don't wake Leroy.

"I'm going to tell you something and I don't want you to freak out or judge me." I hear quiet excitement in Gwen's soft voice. "But after I got your text yesterday...I don't know. I think you play a part in this somehow."

"Okay," I encourage after she pauses too long.

"You know how I go to dialysis three days a week?"

"Mmhmm."

"Erinn, I am getting off the chair. I can't go back there, relying on that machine to keep me alive. I want my body to die naturally."

Now I am wide awake.

Her voice rushes, afraid I will try to talk her out of it before I hear her. "I have almost done this before. Four times, actually. Each time I hear from you, within a day, and then little things happen that make me change my mind. I guess that means you are four-for-four. Which is amazing." Her nervous laugh bubbles across the air waves. "I realized today that before now I wanted to do this out of anger at God or at the clinic. But this time I didn't even make a cognitive decision. The time came

11

for me to leave for dialysis and I was just like, 'No. Not anymore. That's it!' I have so much peace about it. Then as I am missing dialysis you sent me that text. Like you knew somehow."

I process. My mouth dries. My heart pounds.

She is asking me to let her die and watch it happen.

"I am not just jumping into this to test Him," she says. "If He heals me, great, but it's okay if that doesn't happen. I want you to know that. God wants to do something different here and you are a part of it. When I think about you, the word 'vessel' comes to me. Whatever He wants to do here, you are the vessel."

Is this courage or insanity?

Gwen hasn't only chosen to die, she has chosen a painful death.

The kidneys remove waste from the blood through filtration and urination. Without this function, toxins and fluid builds in the bloodstream.

When kidneys fail they require either a total transplant or constant dialysis. The dialysis machine removes toxins through drawing blood, filtering it in a specialized tube and returning it to the body clean with excess fluid removed.

Three days a week, Gwen spends five hours hooked to that machine or she will die. She will be poisoned to death or die from the fluid overwhelming her lungs or heart, causing suffocation or cardiac arrest. That is what she is choosing.

"Erinn?"

"I'm here, just thinking. What did your son say about this?"

"Ethan doesn't know, he would try to talk me out of it. No one else knows. You are the only one who would understand. My family and other friends are afraid of death; they don't know Jesus."

Jesus?

He opens a drawer in my spirit and hands me the map. I know what to do.

"How long do the doctors say you have?"

"Two weeks. No, 11 days now. I have my will and financial stuff taken care of. Today I got my affairs in order with hospice. They will come when the pain gets too bad."

"Come to my house on the days you did dialysis." I am resolved. "I will pray over you. Like we're doing spiritual dialysis instead of physical. Can you do that? I will come to you if you can't."

"I can come. I can do that."

"I need a few days to wrap my head around this. Can we start Friday?"

"Let's do it. Friday!"

Gwen hangs up, but I hold the phone to my ear for another moment. Still processing. This task overwhelms in a tidal wave. Any hardness in my heart toward Gwen breaks down under the comprehension of the painful separation of death.

If she passes, how will I explain it to Leroy? What about her grandson and her son? She isn't giving them a chance to say good-bye.

Though I can't deny the change I heard in her voice. For the first time, Gwen was joyful. Not temporary happiness, real joy laced each word she spoke. Pride swells amidst my grief; she is ready to leave misery behind and has taken drastic measures for this change. She is right. Something new began today.

I am up for hours seeking the face of Jesus. Pacing my house in tears until His still small voice settles me.

I will fight for you, you need only be still. He says.

You are El Shaddai, the Almighty. You are Jehovah-Rapha, the Lord who heals and restores. You are Abba, our Father, ever present in times of trouble. 'Whom shall I fear?'

I go before you. Do not be afraid.

I am the truth-bringer. I am the salt of the earth. I am both servant and warrior for the Living God. I will fight with You for a better ending, Lord. Our hope rests in You and I know Your heart desires life!

It is not over yet.

No. it's not over.

Desperation.

I should have seen this coming. Gwen is not shy about sharing how much she hates her treatments.

She hates the implant and fistula in her arm, surgical changes they made to her veins and artery to make the process of dialysis easier. It is a constant reminder of her diagnosis and a symbol of her reliance on that machine. Her body rejected it for weeks, giving her painful swollen bruises.

She hates the day she made friends with another patient because she never saw him again, and no one could tell her what became of him. No one needed to. She knows how this road ends.

She hates the downcast eyes of the other people hooked to machines.

She hates herself for putting up with it.

She hates that God is allowing this to happen.

"He is so mean," she told me weeks ago. "I tried to pray and all that came out was, *I thought you liked me, Jesus. I thought I was your friend.*' I'm so mad at Him. My heart is broken. This is my life now."

I searched for a word of life or truth to share with her. "I can't tell you why these things happen. I can tell you He is love and He is good. You say this is your life, but your identity is found in God, not your sickness." The words fall on deaf ears. Gwen wanted only to despair, not to be encouraged.

Most of all Gwen hates the dialysis clinic. Its impersonal, spiritual darkness whispers *"Make a fortune from other's misfortune."*

Enduring the treatment was miserable enough but worse, Gwen received no kindness or respect from the staff.

"I am herded through with other human-cattle." Gwen's voice had cracked in anger and sorrow when she explained her dialysis experiences. "I'm there all day three days a week, and even a 'hello' from staff is forced. Maybe I shouldn't expect people to want to talk to me, they're working, but some gentleness would go a long way. They drain seven pounds of water from my sick body and when I finish I feel like a bag of dried up sticks. Then without rest, I am herded out, so the next wave of cattle can come through."

Bitterness shadowed her face when she spoke about the clinic's director and how he enjoys sharing details of his wealth with patients. Gwen listened to this boasting while gritting her teeth, mind wrestling fears of losing her home. "At least someone profits from my distress," she mused.

These suffering people rely on government funding, many with a foot in poverty. Yet they have learned the lavish square footage of the director's home, the make and model of his high-end car, and the duties of his housekeeper.

Last week at dialysis her attendant admitted the employees received a new policy from the corporate office. This policy directed them to teach fitter patients how to unhook themselves from the dialysis equipment in case of an emergency evacuation — for example, a fire, shooting, flash flood.

Gwen is among the few capable enough to learn how to disconnect herself without help. Many patients are confined to wheelchairs due to their frailty, some even missing limbs. What about those people? How would they get out?

While Gwen's attendant instructed her on removing herself, he also revealed the fine print of the new policy. In case of an emergency, medical personnel are not obligated to help patients evacuate. They can just leave them stuck to the machines and get themselves to safety — even knowing that a patient might bleed to death if separated from the machine improperly.

I hope she misunderstood what the attendant told her, but in this world the value of Self is often placed higher than the value of the Other.[3]

Gwen is proof of the destructive power this belief system holds. She would rather die than be worthless.

Your Old Men Shall Dream Dreams.

I dream Gwen throws a party to celebrate her life. I arrive early to pray for her, but many people are already setting up. We sit and begin to pray but there are too many distractions to go deeper.

Party goers soon fill the space and I lose Gwen in the crowd. I realize she hides down the hall of her home, but now the hallway is roped off in three sections by different elements.

The first, at the opening of the hall, hangs a scratchy rope. It is greasy brown and yellow, threads splinter and pierce. The rope displays two knots in the center.

Further down the hall I see the second section begins in a royal blue ribbon with two knots on the left side.

The final section at the end of the hall is marked by a green ribbon the color of new leaves in spring. It exhibits a knot on the left and another on the right. Behind it I see a closed door on the right side.

I speak to a cryptic nurse on the other side of the brown rope, asking for Gwen. She confirms Gwen is down the hallway, but she will not allow me to pass. Sudden and painful, the truth is revealed.

Gwen has chosen death by medically assisted suicide and this nurse will administer the drugs in a moment.

I look to the faces of people gathered. It becomes clear this party is not to celebrate Gwen's life, but to celebrate her death.

Urgent, I find my mother, mother-in-law, father, and father-in-law amongst the crowd. They are drunk and distracted.

"Look at me!" I yell three times.

I grab my mother's hand. "Mom, everyone came here to see Gwen die. We have to leave right now." She sobers and follows me out, along with my mother-in-law and the fathers.

I know this dream is more than neurological musings in the night. The Almighty formed it. I spend the day in pursuit of His Spirit, and study His Word, until He reveals a clear interpretation.

The world celebrates death. It hungers for Gwen's. Do not come into agreement with this mentality, set yourself apart. He says.

The blocked hallway symbolizes Gwen's path from life to death.

The knots in the scratchy brown rope are strongholds.4 They must unravel for her to reach the blue ribbon. This blue ribbon symbolizes My gift of healing5 and I have shown you knots on the left side to signify My power made perfect in human weakness.6

The final ribbon at the end of the hallway shines green. It is the gift of abundance in life. I placed knots on each side to show you the choices given to Gwen over her life. She may choose early death, or she may receive My healing and finish her race.7

The mothers are My church. My bride. Fathers are your mentors. I have called you to get their attention and lead them far from this agreement with death.[8]

Okay, great. That's only a little alarming.

I just need to identify deep rooted strongholds within Gwen and unravel them. Oh, and don't agree with her imminent death. Instead encourage her to finish her race. Then get her and the entire church to understand the difference between facing death versus coming into agreement with death. No pressure, right?

Part I Scriptures

1) Isaiah 45:2 I will go before you and make the crooked places straight. I will break in pieces the gates of brass and cut in sunder the bars of iron.

2) 1 Kings 19:11-12 And he said, Go forth, and stand upon the mount before the Lord. And, behold, the Lord passed by, and a great and strong wind rent the mountains, and brake in pieces the rocks before the Lord; but the Lord was not in the wind: and after the wind an earthquake; but the Lord was not in the earthquake. And after the earthquake a fire; but the Lord was not in the fire: and after the fire a still small voice.

3) Matthew 22:35-40 Then one of them, which was a lawyer, asked him a question, tempting him, and saying, Master, which is the great commandment in the law? Jesus said unto him, Thou shalt love the Lord thy God with all thy heart, and with all thy soul, and with all thy mind. This is the first and great commandment. And the second is like unto it, Thou shalt love thy neighbour as thyself. On these two commandments hang all the law and the prophets.

4) 2 Corinthians 10:3-5 For though we walk in the flesh, we do not war after the flesh: For the weapons of our warfare are not carnal, but mighty through God to the pulling down of strong holds; Casting down imaginations, and every high thing that exalteth itself against the knowledge of God, and bringing into captivity every thought to the obedience of Christ.

5) 2 Corinthians 12:8 And he (the Lord) said unto me, My grace is sufficient for thee: for my strength is made perfect in weakness. Most gladly therefore will I rather glory in my infirmities, that the power of Christ may rest upon me.

6) Proverbs 20:30 The blueness of a wound cleanseth away evil: so do stripes the inward parts of the belly.

7) Hebrews 12:1-2 Wherefore seeing we also are compassed about with so great a cloud of witnesses, let us lay aside every weight, and the sin which doth so easily beset us, and let us run with patience the race that is set before us, Looking unto Jesus the author and finisher of our faith; who for the joy that was set before him endured the cross, despising the shame, and is set down at the right hand of the throne of God.

8) Isaiah 28:16-18 Therefore thus saith the Lord God, Behold, I lay in Zion for a foundation a stone, a tried stone, a precious corner stone, a sure foundation: he that believeth shall not make haste. Judgment also will I lay to the line, and righteousness to the plummet: and the hail shall sweep away the refuge of lies, and the waters shall overflow the hiding place. And your covenant with death shall be disannulled, and your agreement with hell shall not stand; when the overflowing scourge shall pass through, then ye shall be trodden down by it.

Part II:

Strange Things Afoot at the Burger Joint

Day 1. Then Just Trust.

I prepare for my first meeting with Gwen for two days.

I call Dee, the leader of my prayer team, a woman who long ago dedicated her life to fighting spiritual battles and claiming healing in the lives of those in distress. Because of snowstorms and a broken car, I haven't seen our team for weeks. My spiritual tank is empty. "I wish I was with you guys. Now more than ever," I say.

She speaks to my isolation. "You are never alone. Our prayers are always with you! Take communion with Gwen," she advises. "She needs to remember what Jesus paid for with His blood. And you must spend time with the Holy Spirit. He will tell you what He wants you to do. Trust Him."

Trust Him. Easy to say, difficult to live.

Friday arrives. Gwen may have only one more Friday left to live.

The morning is overcast, quiet winter light spills in through the front window. I set Leroy's blue toddler slide in the living room and show him how to send toys down. *That should give me a few minutes.*

I carry my computer to the kitchen counter and stare at the screen.

An agenda, Lord. I want an agenda for today. What is my purpose here? What do You need from me?

I hear Gwen's voice, full of trust, reverberate through my spirit. "You are the vessel," she said.

I'm just me. Who am I to be a vessel for You? I resisted every time You called me to this woman, and I'm the best You've got for a vessel?

His answer is a resolute Spirit settling over me. I start typing, an agenda forms as if predetermined.

It wasn't.

At least not by me.

1. Fellowship. Ask questions to uncover the strongholds. Listen more than talk.
2. Play instrumental worship music while reading Scripture aloud.
3. Lay hands on Gwen.₁ Pray for healing, hope, and a joyful ending.
4. Worship together.
5. Test for any physical responses to spiritual changes. *"Here's a tissue. Wipe those tears. Go to the bathroom; you need to go pee, Gwen!"*
6. Take communion.
7. More fellowship. Allow her as much time to hang out as she wants.
    Above.

I read over what I outlined. Seven steps. God is a show-off. Seven is a numerical theme in God's word. He uses it as a sign of divine perfection, spiritual completion, and rest.2

My eyes travel back over my second task.

'Read Scripture.' I need Scriptures!

I panic. There is only one hour before Gwen's arrival and it will probably take the entire time to look up verses. But in ten minutes the agenda is in my computer and complete. It contains 20 minutes of Scripture from various books of the Holy Bible. I decide to remove the verse references. I want to read Gwen the word of God without interruption, giving her an endless stream of His truth.

I jump around my house, a fizzling ball of nerves. I chastise myself for this anxiety. I minister to people every Monday with my prayer team. We pray over people from all walks of life for all forms of suffering. This should not feel any different.

Why is it different?

"You are alone." A slippery voice whispers, igniting the fire of my fears. I remember what my mentor Dee said. "I am not alone," I say aloud. "The Lord of Heaven and His church are with me." The fear vanishes and the doorbell rings.

Gwen blows in with her pajamas still on under a thick grey coat. She holds out a beautiful fringed shawl. "I want to give you this. It is hand-made. It cost me a stupid amount of money when I bought it. I just couldn't resist the soft yarn! When I tried it on at home, I realized it looked like a blanket swallowed me whole." She demonstrates, putting her small hands through the arm holes and dropping the fabric around her.

I laugh. "Yeah, maybe it isn't supposed to cover the ground like that."

"I saw it this morning and I imagined you holding your son with it wrapped around you both. You're perfect for it."

I run my fingertips over the knitted shawl's silken yarn. "Thank you, I love it."

We move into my home amidst wagging tails, and joyful, outstretched toddler hands. We sit at my kitchen table and fellowship over a warm cup of peach and chamomile tea.

Gwen is excited when I tell her about my dream. "And then God said the knots on the blue ribbon symbolize His power made perfect in weakness." I grin with childlike wonder. "Gwen, you may be at the end of your life, but you go out with a bang, not a whisper. You may be at your weakest, but now you rise stronger than ever through the power of Jesus!"

We finish our tea and I send her to the couch. I find the computer still at rest on the kitchen counter, turn up the music, and begin praying the Scriptures over her.

My voice rises above the melody. No longer just me, I become a vessel of the Holy Spirit. A reverse waterfall — my feet the cliffs, and out from my mouth come roaring the waters of Niagara.

Not one of those words flowing from me is my own, rather ancient holy truth from a mighty God. Thousand-year-old words as alive today as the moment God breathed them into the penholder.

What an incredible God.

The torrent of His words pulls Gwen from the couch and when I finish reading she is face down, prostrate on my living room rug, between the toddler slide and my second-hand couch.

I anoint her head with oil and lay hands on her back to pray.[3]

The Holy Spirit sets me aflame, heat rises on my face and hands. I burn, it's like lightning crackles through my bones. I shake within, but my hands remain steady.

Mostly steady.

The strangeness causes me to expect healing or deliverance to manifest for Gwen right away. It isn't until later this night that I realize He activated something in me.

Leroy leaves his car game. He examines Gwen then looks to my face to determine the normality of all this. I smile, "Sometimes crying is a good thing, Bubbies." He sits next to me and places his tiny hands on her back beside my own. Together we worship before the throne of heaven from the floor of my living room.

The songs fade into silence, and the time comes for Gwen to stand. Snot and tears run down her cheeks. Gwen covers her face with her hands and apologizes.

I wave it off, "That's normal, considering the circumstances. A little snot helps keep us grounded!" I hear her still laughing when the bathroom door shuts.

The ability to empty her bladder could mean healthy kidney function. The sign of a miracle. "Were you able to pee?" I ask, when she resurfaces.

"Nothing out of the ordinary." Gwen says without disappointment. Her face glows with refreshed joy.

We take communion and she is eager to learn how vital the bread and cup are to believers. "It is the reminder that Jesus paid the price for sin, sickness, and death at the cross. It brings health and wholeness when we understand what belongs to us through His blood," I explain. "It is so important, that according to Paul, when the church of Corinth lost understanding of communion it caused sickness and death." 4 I give Gwen extra grape juice and crackers to take home with her.

"I have lived as a Christian for 30 years and no one ever prayed over me like that. Thank you. Thank you so much." Gwen marvels as I walk her to the door.

Humbled, I deflect the praise. I am just me again. Without the Spirit of the Lord, I was only reading an old book and making a bunch of noise.

Gwen leaves ready to slay giants. I watch her white car pull out the driveway and sway on my feet. Every part of me drained. I resolve not to cook dinner and instead grab burgers to make the rest of my day easier.

I didn't realize then, but my day was far from over.

Day 1. Tested by Fire.

Only 11:30 a.m. Gwen just left the house ablaze. I wonder how many cups of coffee it will take to get me moving again.

Leroy goes down for a nap, it is time to try getting some work done. I am a telemarketer. Yes. A telemarketer. I have this spirit-filled morning then I head upstairs to cold call unsuspecting office workers and sell them copier supplies.

Proof of God's strange sense of humor. The strangest part of the day is still to come.

Evening falls and dinner calls. I cannot put two thoughts together, so when my husband gets home I make a quick trip to the local burger joint. It's packed.

After placing my order, I retreat to wait at a table outside. The cool night air and quiet evening provide a safe space to at last reflect on my dramatic morning. Leaning back, my eyes drink in the stars growing brighter in the darkening sky.

Look. I hear His voice.

What am I looking at? Will You send me a shooting star?

Look.

I straighten and peer into the restaurant. An older woman makes her way to the door with her arms full of burger meal bags.

What in the...?

I see into her. Like an x-ray. A mass of glowing red light surrounds her left shoulder; clinging to joint and bone like sticky glue.

Her shoulder is in pain. When she comes out, stop her and pray over it.

So . . . I leap to the door. The moment she steps out of the restaurant, I pray for the healing of her shoulder with confidence and divine authority!

No. That is not what happens.

. . . I stand. I open the door for her, wishing her a good night with a "God bless you!"

No. That doesn't happen either.

Ever the brave and bold soul, I plant my feet and grip the chair. *Don't make me do this. Please. Not here. I'm not doing this here.* I bite my tongue to keep my mouth shut as the poor woman passes. I stare holes into the sidewalk as she leaves with her shoulder still in pain.

Not a smile for her. Not a "Good evening." I didn't even open the door, despite my knowledge of her pain and her full arms.

34

Shamefaced, I shrink back inside, hoping my food is ready. I want this failure behind me, buried deep under French Fries.

But when I pass the threshold I see everything. Every ache, every pain, every sorrow. Each person I look at, I see into their bodies and their hearts.

She has a thyroid problem.

That unequally yoked couple needs to separate because she is called to serve hurting children and he will hold her back.

Jealousy is causing uncontrollable anger in this man, destroying his relationships.

It doesn't stop. I can't close my eyes because I see apart from eyesight. I can't look away because people are everywhere. Everyone hurts with sickness and brokenness.

This couple loves each other but their marriage is under attack.

The cashier doesn't know he is developing a heart condition.

This is what a psychotic episode looks like! I am crazy, having a mental breakdown. My son will grow up with Wacko Mom. Oh, Lord, how do I know this isn't a mental breakdown?

The only way to know is to ask. Ask her. Peace. She needs peace. The Lord Jesus nudges my heart as a young woman approaches. We are close in age, late twenties. Silken, sandy colored hair cropped short meets her shoulders. With soft eyes and an easy smile, she slips through the crowded room.

Is there a way to run from someone without offending them? Nope. I don't think so. Please don't ask this of me!

She smiles and gestures to the chair across from me. "Is this seat taken? I am just here for a to-go order."

"I was actually about to get up so you're welcome to it!" Rising, I try to move away, but bodies block all means of escape. I cannot go forward, and I cannot go backward. Standing in the aisle, I avoid eye contact with this young woman, but her presence is tangible.

The Lord reminds me of all the years I prayed for people and spoke in agreement with His Word. **Are you going to talk about this or are you going to act on it?**

That was different. I was in the safety of my church. Isn't that different?

Do you believe?

I bow my head. *Yes, Jesus. I believe.*

Do you really believe what I am capable of? Do you really believe in Me?

I do, Jesus, I believe.

Then step out.5

"You know what, I will sit here." My fingers get wiggly in my lap. I rock back and forth. I throw glances at her. Spit it out! "Umm. I have an odd thing to ask you. Are you anxious about something that I can pray for peace over you right now?"

. . . Those soft eyes flash. She is offended. She calls me a psycho and leaves without her food. Everyone in the restaurant boos while I ugly-sob into a chocolate shake.

No. Of course that didn't happen. Because I am not crazy. I am a child of the Living God. I gave my life to Him to serve who He asks me to, speak what He says, see what He sees, and believe the unbelievable.

Her name is Beth and she does need peace. She is anxious because she is at a crossroads regarding her career path. Taking her hands in mine, I pray for an increase of peace. The words force their way out and my 'Amen' is abrupt.

My food order comes up moments after we finish praying. I thank Beth for her open-mindedness and rush out with food I no longer feel like eating.

As I drive home I realize God wanted to share more with Beth through me. I gave Him no chance, but I hear the words now as I try to quiet myself. He wanted me to say: *"Beth, you will succeed no matter what path you take. A spirit of joy lies within and because of this joy you find favor with others. Don't be afraid because as long as the steps you take glorify God, your path comes into alignment with His calling on your life."*

37

I didn't say it because I lost to fear and human insecurity.

Back in my home, the burger bag swings forgotten in my fist as I, wild-eyed, recount my supernatural crazy-town trip to my husband.

Tylor is not even a little surprised. "This is what you asked for." He says, rescuing the to-go bag from my flailing hands and biting into his burger as if this is a regular family dinner.

His nonchalance infuriates me. I sputter weak arguments, but my voice falls on deaf ears as Tylor feeds Leroy crispy fries. He's right and we both know it. Last week I told him the desire of my heart was to give Living Water₆ to those who need it, no matter the circumstances.

My exact words, *"No matter the circumstances."*

Yep. That's enough for me today.

My head aches from all the mind blowing; I withdraw to a cool, dark room to recover.

Day 3. Hitting the Target.

The King takes me to a hilltop within my spirit as I pray. We sit looking out at green fields encased in morning light and I lean on Him to recover from the growing pains. I come to Him convicted and He anointed me in abundant mercy. He is a good and patient teacher.

Will you give me another chance to pray over the woman's shoulder? And Beth. Can I see her again and tell her Your promise about her career path? I pray.

I don't want to leave the house, but the baby needs diapers. I'm terrified as I drive to the store, afraid of it happening again and even more afraid of it never happening again.

He draws me close, holding my hand. **Don't be afraid, child. Look. What do you see?** I try to look *into* the people I pass. I do not see something for everyone, like I did at the restaurant. I see a flicker of a vision or hear a word. Jesus walks serene beside me, directing me around the crowds.

He struggles with sobriety. Pray for him about it.

Offer a blessing over this family here.

This woman conceals a battle with depression.

Maybe this voice I hear is my own, a product of wishful thinking.

As I head to the check out, He addresses my fears again, reminding me the only way to confirm the truth is to step out.

I set my basket on the checkout counter and see the girl working this lane. Skin soft and pale, glowing against black hair pulled into a messy bun. Straight strands fall into her round face as she bags another customer's items. I feel her emotional weariness. Her spirit says, "*I am invisible. Do I matter?*" The love Jesus holds for her warms me. With great pride He tells me, **She is My talented artist. Ask her about her art.**

My eyes scan for signs of paint, smudging, anything to start the conversation. Nothing. "Can I ask you something?" She nods, eyes lowered. "Are you an artist?"

Her chin comes up. Shoulders straighten. Eyes brighten and meet mine with confidence. "Yes. Yes, I am!" She tells me of her passion for many artistic mediums. She experiments with charcoal on canvas to produce images that look like ultrasounds. "I just created one for my mom. She overcame cancer and I wanted to show her how proud I am of her fight so, I depicted her in one of my pieces. It's like she is a new person about to enter into a different life." She gets embarrassed and notices other customers listening. Her voice trails off, but I nod encouragement.

"Like an unborn baby," I say.

She grins, revealing a charming gap in her front teeth. "Yeah! Like an unborn baby. She's my hero."

"You need to do a complete series like this, in ultrasound. It will impact more people than you realize." The prophetic words never process in my brain and they heat my body as they form on my tongue. "Keep up the good work!"

My heart turns to God in praise as I leave. "Thank you, Jesus. What a blessing to see the change in Your artist," I tell Him as I grab Leroy's diapers and head to the car. "Thank you, Lord, for seeing all of us.₇ Even when we don't see ourselves. Only you, Father, chooses a telemarketer to speak words of life₈ to a checkout girl!"

Cool right?!

But what about Gwen?

Tomorrow we pray again. Tomorrow she might have only five days left.

Part II Scriptures

1) Mark 16:17-18 And these signs shall follow them that believe; In my name shall they cast out devils; they shall speak with new tongues; They shall take up serpents; and if they drink any deadly thing, it shall not hurt them; they shall lay hands on the sick, and they shall recover.

2) Psalm 12:6 The words of the Lord are pure words: as silver tried in a furnace of earth, purified seven times.

3) James 5:14-16 Is any sick among you? let him call for the elders of the church; and let them pray over him, anointing him with oil in the name of the Lord: And the prayer of faith shall save the sick, and the Lord shall raise him up; and if he have committed sins, they shall be forgiven him. Confess your faults one to another, and pray one for another, that ye may be healed. The effectual fervent prayer of a righteous man availeth much.

4) 1 Corinthians 11:20-32 When you come together, it is not the Lord's supper that you eat. For in eating, each one goes ahead with his own meal. One goes hungry, another gets drunk. What! Do you not have houses to eat and drink in? Or do you despise the church of God and humiliate those who have nothing? What shall I say to you? Shall I commend you in this? No, I will not. For I received from the Lord what I also delivered to you, that the Lord Jesus on the night when he was betrayed took bread, and when he had given thanks, he broke it, and said, "This is

my body, which is for you. Do this in remembrance of me." In the same way also he took the cup after supper, saying, "This cup is the new covenant in my blood. Do this, as often as you drink it, in remembrance of me." For as often as you eat this bread and drink the cup, you proclaim the Lord's death until he comes. Whoever, therefore, eats the bread or drinks the cup of the Lord in an unworthy manner will be guilty concerning the body and blood of the Lord. Let a person examine himself, then, and so eat of the bread and drink of the cup. For anyone who eats and drinks without discerning the body eats and drinks judgment on himself. That is why many of you are weak and ill, and some have died. But if we judged ourselves truly, we would not be judged. But when we are judged by the Lord, we are disciplined so that we may not be condemned along with the world.

5) Matthew 14:22-33 And straightway Jesus constrained his disciples to get into a ship, and to go before him unto the other side, while he sent the multitudes away. And when he had sent the multitudes away, he went up into a mountain apart to pray: and when the evening was come, he was there alone. But the ship was now in the midst of the sea, tossed with waves: for the wind was contrary. And in the fourth watch of the night Jesus went unto them, walking on the sea. And when the disciples saw him walking on the sea, they were troubled, saying, It is a spirit; and they cried out for fear. But straightway Jesus spake unto them, saying, Be of good cheer; it is

I; be not afraid. And Peter answered him and said, Lord, if it be thou, bid me come unto thee on the water. And he said, Come. And when Peter was come down out of the ship, he walked on the water, to go to Jesus. But when he saw the wind boisterous, he was afraid; and beginning to sink, he cried, saying, Lord, save me. And immediately Jesus stretched forth his hand, and caught him, and said unto him, O thou of little faith, wherefore didst thou doubt? And when they were come into the ship, the wind ceased. Then they that were in the ship came and worshipped him, saying, Of a truth thou art the Son of God.

6) John 7:37-39 In the last day, that great day of the feast, Jesus stood and cried, saying, If any man thirst, let him come unto me, and drink. He that believeth on me, as the Scripture hath said, out of his belly shall flow rivers of living water. (But this spake he of the Spirit, which they that believe on him should receive: for the Holy Ghost was not yet given; because that Jesus was not yet glorified.)

7) Psalm 139 1- 6 O lord, thou hast searched me, and known me. Thou knowest my downsitting and mine uprising, thou understandest my thought afar off. Thou compassest my path and my lying down, and art acquainted with all my ways. For there is not a word in my tongue, but, lo, O Lord, thou knowest it altogether. Thou hast beset me behind and before and laid thine hand upon me. Such knowledge is too

wonderful for me; it is high, I cannot attain unto it.

8) Proverbs 18:20-21 A man's belly shall be satisfied with the fruit of his mouth; and with the increase of his lips shall he be filled. Death and life are in the power of the tongue: and they that love it shall eat the fruit thereof.

Part III:

Torches Pass on a Snowy Day

Day 4. Knots.

Snow falls in thick fluffy flakes coating the streets and lawns, encasing me in a peaceful snow globe. I worry Gwen won't make it out, but right on time her car pulls up.

My heart breaks anew when Gwen's son, Ethan, steps out to open her door. She told him, and he came. He is not a believer in Jesus, making his presence here an act of pure love.

I know a lot about him while he knows nothing of me. Ethan is an only child reared by a single mother, (Gwen avoids the topic of his father). Broad shouldered and tough looking, Gwen glows over Ethan. He is the greatest achievement of her life. She has shared that he is a hard worker, trusted by his boss to get the job done right. He has a clever five-year-old son of his own.

Ethan meets the dogs' enthusiastic greetings with a generous amount of petting. I wrestle the two beasts and introduce myself amid apologies. "It's okay, I have three dogs," Ethan smiles and shrugs. "Mom probably told you, but our female just had pups. We are buried under animals at my house."

"Sounds like my kind of place!" I say, glad to have common ground. "It is perfect weather for snuggling with a pile of puppies."

The three of us find chairs at the kitchen table and I discern what topic needs immediate attention. Gwen's body has maybe a week before giving out; the time for gentle probing is over.

I address the root issues keeping her from receiving healing. I think of the knots in the brown rope from my dream. Two strongholds. Two tight-wound reasons Gwen cannot move forward. After prayerful pursuit, I call these strongholds out of hiding:

Lie #1: If Gwen lives, she will lose her home. She can bring more value to her son dead because he inherits her house.

The Truth: Stuff suffocates when placed too high in worth. What once was a blessing is worthless when it separates us from God, the provider of all needs and wants.1

Lie #2: Gwen's overwhelming loneliness has made her believe there is no longer a benefit to her existence. No one will miss her when she is gone, and she offers nothing else of worth to the world.

The Truth: Being alone does not equal being unloved or unneeded. The enemy of life is a clever hunter, working to alienate people from one another. When an individual separates from the group, she becomes easier prey.2 Sickness does not equal worthlessness. Each person has a purpose and a destiny. This world brings strife, but these struggles do not give us a pass on our calling.3 The Lord asked Peter to get out of the boat in the middle of a storm, not when the waves were calm.

I pause, hopeful that uncovering these issues in front of Ethan educates him regarding the seriousness of his mother's fight and gives him the chance to soothe her fears.

Gwen is nodding, she agrees these are the reasons she chooses death, but she deafens herself to the arguments against them. Our conversation takes many turns and I struggle to keep the focus.

Ethan asks thoughtful questions about Christian beliefs in a soft, respectful voice. We talk about miracles of modern medicine and Ethan questions his mother for not seeking such a miracle by getting on a waiting list for a kidney transplant. "Can't you just call? I gave you the number and then you did nothing with it."

"I'm not going off dialysis to test God into healing me," she deflects. Ethan has yet to comprehend what I knew all along. Gwen does not *want* to live.

With the truth concealed, we cannot move forward. "Gwen, we'll start reading Scripture and praying in a minute. I have a question but don't answer yet. I want you to examine your heart with Jesus while we pray. Do you want to be healed and live, or do you want to go home to be with the Lord?"

Gwen meets my eyes and I see she already knows the answer. I hope she changes her mind. "Okay. I'll meditate on it," she says.

Ethan and his mama get comfortable on my loveseat. I turn on worship music and begin to read as doubts nip at my heart. *I bet Ethan thinks this is cheesy. This all must seem bizarre. Is the instrumental music weird? Maybe I shouldn't have used it this time. I wish I put the slide away and picked up more toys. How silly to do this with kid stuff scattered everywhere.*

I declare the Scriptures louder, my voice smothering insecurities.

Ethan and Gwen huddle in a tight love ball. When I finish the Scriptures, I lay hands on them both and pray for healing to flow from the heart of the Father.

When Gwen excuses herself to blow her nose, I look to Ethan for feedback. "What you did, it was powerful," he says. Shame on me for doubting the supremacy of God's Word. Ancient God-breathed Holy Scriptures, and I worried it sounded cheesy.

Then Ethan admits he was concerned about coming, thinking he would be asked to pray aloud. He pulls his grandfather's rosary from under his shirt, a classic crucifix dangles from his hands. I see the metallic Christ's head hanging from the weight of His sacrifice before Ethan lets Him drop. "I wore this to honor my grandpa and, I don't know. I felt like it was all I could offer." His hand rests on the cross, "I realized once you started, your job was to pray and my job to hold my mom."

Praise to Everlasting God!

Jesus has knocked on the door of this man's heart and he seems unaware of it.4 Even if someone denies the Lord entry, they can still hear His voice.

Gwen comes down the stairs, delighted eyes on her son. I wonder if she eavesdropped.

I will no longer allow her to conceal the truth. "Do you want to be healed? Or do you want to go home?"

Serene and somber, Gwen studies her son's face. "I want to go home. I'm sorry," she admits. "if God wants to heal me, He still can."

It's not what Ethan nor I want, but the truth is out. "You think God would force healing against your will?"

Ethan reflects on a topic we discussed before prayer regarding the words of Jesus, ***"The harvest is plentiful, but the workers are few."*** 5 "So you are someone out working the harvest for your Father, right?" He asks his mother, "Do you think a Father forces a child to stay working the harvest? When their hands bleed, they are tired, and begging to come inside? I would not want that for my kid. I would let him come back in."

Difficult logic to deny. But the infinite extent of God's love is beyond reason.

As they discuss this concept my mind wanders. Before Gwen's decree of death, I imagined the impact of healed Gwen's testimony. Now I see the world without her and I refuse to tolerate unfinished work, so I make a proclamation. "I know you are not done with what you came here to do, Gwen. I don't believe it's your appointed time to die.6 Whatever you need to finish, I will finish. Whatever gifts left unlocked within you become my gifts. Whoever waits for you to witness to them, I will tell them the good news. I promise right now in Jesus' name, I take up what you leave behind."

Gwen takes my hand and we make a covenant. If she taps out early, I take over her path alongside my own. She likens this to the prophet Elijah and his acolyte Elisha in 2 Kings Chapter 2 of the Bible.7 Her eyes alight with excitement, she recounts the story of two men of God: Elijah who is ready to enter the kingdom of heaven, and Elisha who asks for the gifts of his teacher after his passing.

As she tells me this story, I see a dull sword cut through the rope of my dream. Not a clean cut. The fabric frays from a careless tear and the pieces with knots intact drift down. They continue falling into a void. A warning. *This is wrong. I leave knots untied.* The King told me not to come into agreement with Gwen's death.

Gwen will be healed in death, if not on earth. There is no sickness in Your Kingdom. I argue. *If she dies, I cannot allow my enemy any further conquest.* The vision repeats. My chest constricts, and I no longer feel satisfied with our covenant. Her early death means Ethan saying good bye to his mother sooner than expected. It means my friend no longer is here to laugh at my son with me or bake me granola cherry tarts.

It means we would never know the healing gift of the blue ribbon.

It is difficult to resist her death. How else can this end?

Just because she chooses death today does not mean this is over. The Father says to my spirit.

Leroy has been bobbing around during the visit. He collected a series of items and placed them in Ethan's lap. Now Ethan tosses a dinosaur, a truck, and a measuring cup into the toy box. Knowing a good Da when he sees one, Leroy lifts his hands up to Ethan as we say goodbyes.

"Can I pick up your son?"

"Of course!"

Once lifted, Leroy gives Ethan the sweetest cuddliest hug. I am sorry you're sad. His chubby baby arms say.

God, prepare Ethan's heart for what comes. May the ears of his spirit continue to turn toward Your voice, and the time left with his mother be blessed. I pray as I watch a son walk his dying mother down a snowy walkway. Will this be the last time I see them together? Lord Jesus, please fix our eyes to Your plan. Not Gwen's or mine or Ethan's. Just You. "A man's heart deviseth his way: but the LORD directeth his steps."8 Halleluiah and Amen.

Day 5. Remember His Goodness.

I hope any parent reading this disagrees, but I am just gonna say it...

My son is the best of all humans.

Small children are wondrous creatures. How special to see them become their own people. I love watching my baby grow into a kid. Leroy's personality develops more each day. I see his quirks now, his jokes, and fears. I love watching him, my little moving masterpiece.

Still, the naughtiness is aplenty. His name changes daily from "The Hurricane" to "Bubbies" or "Goobery Schmoobis".

"What is in your mouth!?" is a common question echoing through the house.

This morning I ask for help from the Most High, exhausted from battling Gwen's desire for death. My overwhelmed heart stands on the precipice of an unexplored cavern.

I have petitioned for many things on this walk with You, Lord, but my prayers have never combated life against death.

Have you forgotten?

The Father sends me after my Goobery Schmoobis, who is ready to put a rock in his mouth.

I laugh at the boy's giggles and catch him for a kiss before he squirms away again. *No, I cannot forget what You have done for me.* Time would not be spent chasing this little person if it weren't for the cries of my heart before the Lord.

I have shared many things with you; now I want to tell you about my child.

I waited 3 years, 9 months, and 15 days for Leroy to exist. Some seasons I walked in patience, content to wait on God's perfect timing. Other seasons I spent begging him with a broken heart. Every month I held tight to hope.

I am little nauseous today. Maybe, just maybe...

I felt exhausted this week. What if...?

3 years, 9 months, and 15 days of watching other people have babies and subsequent babies. I wish I could get all my money back on those countless negative pregnancy tests.

Hope is a painful gift and it brought me to my knees.

During my third year of barrenness I sacrificed a familiar prayer to my Creator.

Thank you, Lord, for Your perfect timing in the life of my child. Please find favor with me to adopt, if that is Your plan. Lord, please comfort my heart as I wait for this baby. I have never wanted something more.

I received an answer loud and clear, yet when it came it was hard to claim.

You will conceive your child within six months. Call your sisters in Christ. Humble yourself and ask for prayer. Tell them I have said six months.

Why ask for prayer, Lord? People already pray for this baby to happen.

So, they share in My Glory when this child is borne. Holy Spirit said, His hand holding my heart. I could feel His joy.

How shameful to admit a broken-heart. How insane to proclaim an imminent pregnancy without any physical sign this can ever happen. But I called up my girls anyway. I couldn't bring myself to tell them "six months". In my doubt, I told them to expect a baby within the year.

Holy Spirit moved through the faith of my loved ones. My husband's grandfather wove two baby paracord bracelets in expectation. My mother cried out in prayer days before I asked her to. My sister-in-law set aside baby clothes and toys from my growing nephews; planning to pass them on to their cousin.

Then there was the night in July with my prayer team.

Each week our prayer team breaks off into smaller ministry teams of twos or threes. This time I was teamed up with a greying bachelor, Dale. In between praying for people, Dale squirmed against something he needed to say to me. He attempted to voice it with odd comments. "Well, you're young and healthy." Later, "Your husband seems nice. A big strong guy, I bet."

Yes, Dale, thank you. Good talk.

When at last he worked up the courage, it went something like this: "So, you got married a while ago, and you're a lovely young woman. I don't mean that in a weird way. I'm trying to say you are beautiful and make a good, um. No. I mean I don't want to say anything inappropriate but…"

My patience dried up. "What's up, Dale? Go ahead and get it out."

The words summersaulted after one another like the Holy Spirit shoved them. "Can I pray over you to get pregnant?"

I never told Dale about my desire to become a mother. The timing of his offer combined with the promise of an imminent pregnancy steadied my wavering faith. "Yes! Please do!"

Dale prayed the most uncomfortable prayer of his life, petitioning the Lord to bless the union of my husband and I with a child. The delightful humor of God. He wanted to use a man childless and unmarried to pray for something he never understood or wished for himself.

With the humility of a faithful servant, Dale obeyed. He prayed for me that day and onward. Over the next two months, he sent emails with Scriptures about women of the Bible once barren and then blessed with children by the hand of God. He inserted my name in these Scriptures where the names of Hannah, Sarah, Elizabeth, and Rebekah once stood. Dale embarked on prayer projects wholeheartedly. His basement transformed into an altar where he spent hours praying late into the night. He fought for me to have my child.

That October I took my first positive pregnancy test in the bathroom of a grocery store because I could not wait until I got home.

My miracle was born in June. A few short days after his birth, Dale passed on to the glory of heaven, surprising us all.

In one of my last conversations with him, I teased Dale about what comes next. "Are you planning to jump out of a plane over the desert? Maybe drop down on nomadic peoples to bless them with The Word?" I said, imagining my wispy haired friend parachuting down to a morning campfire in the middle of nowhere, preaching the good news as he descends.

Dale always had a mission planned. He often served in prison ministry, our healing prayer team ministry, and many adventures taking him over the sea. His most recent trip was three-weeks of traveling with gypsies in eastern Europe.

"I don't feel God calling me into anything right now." Dale said, thoughtfully rubbing his knee.

But God did call upon Dale's heart for a final mission — to help pray into life a baby boy with a big destiny.

When I pull Leroy from his crib in the morning, I marvel at the power of prayer. I hold a human being in my hands because Jesus made a way for me to kneel before God and ask Him for life. Jesus made a way for Dale to step up beside me, on a final quest.

I believe my son is destined to the same adventurous ministry Dale was. He carries on the torch Dale left behind. He will one day sacrifice hours at the altar interceding for the cries of another's heart.

My son proves God listens when we cry out to Him and moves in ways we cannot fully see or understand.9

I stand on this truth as I battle for the life of my beloved Gwendolynn. *Thank you for reminding me, My King.*

Part III Scriptures

1) Matthew 7:7-11 Ask, and it shall be given you; seek, and ye shall find; knock, and it shall be opened unto you: For every one that asketh receiveth; and he that seeketh findeth; and to him that knocketh it shall be opened. Or what man is there of you, whom if his son ask bread, will he give him a stone? Or if he ask a fish, will he give him a serpent?

2) Mark 3:24-25 And if a kingdom be divided against itself, that kingdom cannot stand. And if a house be divided against itself, that house cannot stand.

3) John 16:33 These things I have spoken unto you, that in me ye might have peace. In the world ye shall have tribulation: but be of good cheer; I have overcome the world.

4) Revelations 3:20 Behold, I stand at the door, and knock: if any man hear my voice, and open the door, I will come in to him, and will sup with him, and he with me.

5) Matthew 9:37 Then saith he unto his disciples, The harvest truly is plenteous, but the labourers are few.

6) Job 22:16 They were cut down before their time, whose foundation was overflown with a flood.

7) 2 Kings 2:6-15 And Elijah said unto him, Tarry, I pray thee, here; for the Lord hath sent me to Jordan. And he said, As the Lord liveth, and as thy soul liveth, I will not leave thee. And they two went on. And fifty men of the sons of the prophets went, and stood to view afar off: and they two stood by Jordan.

And Elijah took his mantle, and wrapped it together, and smote the waters, and they were divided hither and thither, so that they two went over on dry ground. And it came to pass, when they were gone over, that Elijah said unto Elisha, Ask what I shall do for thee, before I be taken away from thee. And Elisha said, I pray thee, let a double portion of thy spirit be upon me. And he said, Thou hast asked a hard thing: nevertheless, if thou see me when I am taken from thee, it shall be so unto thee; but if not, it shall not be so. And it came to pass, as they still went on, and talked, that, behold, there appeared a chariot of fire, and horses of fire, and parted them both asunder; and Elijah went up by a whirlwind into heaven. And Elisha saw it, and he cried, My father, my father, the chariot of Israel, and the horsemen thereof. And he saw him no more: and he took hold of his own clothes, and rent them in two pieces. He took up also the mantle of Elijah that fell from him, and went back, and stood by the bank of Jordan; And he took the mantle of Elijah that fell from him, and smote the waters, and said, Where is the Lord God of Elijah? and when he also had smitten the waters, they parted hither and thither: and Elisha went over. And when the sons of the prophets which were to view at Jericho saw him, they said, The spirit of Elijah doth rest on Elisha. And they came to meet him, and bowed themselves to the ground before him.

8) Proverbs 16:9 A man's heart deviseth his way: but the Lord directeth his steps.

9) Isaiah 65:24 And it shall come to pass, that before they call, I will answer; and while they are yet speaking, I will hear.

Part IV:

The New Normal

Day 6. We Record a Testimony.

Wednesday. Three days left?

"What did Ethan think? Has he said anything?" I ask Gwen at our next prayer session.

She laughs. "Yep. When we got back in the car after the other day, he said 'Well, Erinn is not F'ing around'."

I set down the kettle, tea-making forgotten. "That's the best F'ing compliment I ever got!"

No. I am not messing around. Everything within me believes this.

Would our ministry be more effective as a church if we convinced non-believers we are not messing around? Our desire for service on earth should not be limited to a Sunday gathering, singing songs and listening to sermons.

We should impact our neighborhoods, our cities, and our world, see the sick healed and the suffering, delivered. We should leave work a better place than when we entered and raise up brave, counter-culture children. We must strive to live the Father-heart of our God, our actions reflecting His active presence.

Ugh, I could monologue on this for hours.

Back to Wednesday.

Gwen has something on her heart. She feels it is time to share the story of a young mother who promised to serve Jesus but failed Him the second He asked something of her.

She grips my attention as I sip my tea and rock Leroy to sleep.

"Once upon a time, as a young girl, I took part in the bullying of another child. Let's call her Suzy, seems like a solid name from the 70s," Gwen begins. *"Other children often preyed on Suzy because of her glasses, acne, wild hair, and fearful temperament. Like a cliché movie, the other girls and I, herded Suzy to a back corner of the playground and verbally assaulted her.*

"Suzy huddled in a ball with her hands over her ears and tears streaming down her face. 'Please! Stop! Go away, please just go away! Stop!' I remember Suzy crying, with eyes shut tight, her head shaking back and forth. I eased to the back of the crowd, feeling the wrongness of the moment. But still laughed along and shouting a few insults of my own.

"Fast forward 20 years. I am the mother of a healthy two-year-old son, engaged to a great guy and I have just received Jesus Christ as my Savior. I worked in downtown Denver at a solid job, proud to be providing well for my little family. One sunny afternoon I found myself on the public steps of downtown after work, taking a moment to praise the Lord for all the blessings in my life. 'I will do anything for You, my dear Jesus. Anything!' I told my Savior.

"God wasted no time with His request. I look up and who do I see after all those years? Here comes Suzy. With heartbreaking pressure, God tells me to seek forgiveness for my cruel part in her

torment. Instead I turned my face to keep Suzy from seeing me. I checked my watch thinking, 'My bus is almost here. I can't miss the bus!'

"I didn't miss the bus, but as I boarded I heard the Lord whisper. 'You said you would do anything. Anything.' I couldn't block the memory He drew forth of that girl, eyes shut tight behind fogged glasses, small hands gripping tiny ears. I no longer heard the other passengers on the bus or the roar of traffic, only Suzy's broken little girl voice: 'Please! Stop! Please!'

"And isn't this human nature though," Gwen says, reflecting with annoyance at her former self. "I felt horrible on that bus ride home. Probably the most convicted I ever felt in my life, but I still let it go, completely forgetting about it. How stupid is that? Until about eight months later…when God gave me another chance. . ."

"Now Ethan is three-years-old, I've married the great guy and am growing daily in my walk with Jesus. I still love my job downtown and rejoice in life with my new family. Again, I find myself on the same steps downtown, praising the Lord for the abundant blessings in my life. 'I will do anything for You, my dear Jesus. Anything!' I tell Him just before I spy a familiar form crossing the street. 'Is that…? I can't believe it. It's her.'

"During those eight months, I matured in faith, the Lord preparing me to meet this second opportunity with courage. 'Suzy!' I called. Suzy stopped walking and frowned in confusion, not recognizing me. I re-introduced myself then cut to the chase.

'I can't forget that horrible day in our childhood.' I said. 'I don't remember how it started, but I still see you against the fence.

About six of us girls surrounded you and tormented you as you cried.' Suzy's arms crossed her chest and she shrugged, nodding. She remembered. 'I am devastated that happened to you. I can't tell you how much I regret my part in it. I wish I defended you. I wish. . .'

'It's alright." Suzy waved my apology off. "We were kids. It's fine.'

"I remember thinking how else can you respond to such a deep scar? 'No. It is not alright. Not then, and not now!' I told her. 'Please, will you forgive me for my involvement?'"

'Really, it's okay.' Suzy stepped away, glancing at her watch. 'It was a long time ago.'

"I gripped her shoulders. 'No! Suzy, you misunderstand. It is not okay. God wants me to ask you for forgiveness for this. He says it is not okay!'

"At last Suzy met my gaze and we hugged, as she gasped and cried 'Thank you. I forgive you. Thank you.'"

Weakened and strengthened by sharing the story, Gwen lays her head back and sinks deeper into the couch. She covers herself in Leroy's thick dragon sleeping bag, the only thing able to keep her warm anymore. "I never saw Suzy again after that day." She gazes at my ceiling with a lingering smile, the memory of God's goodness lighting her eyes.

I'm overwhelmed by another example of redemption and obedience. God desires to mend the brokenness within, no matter how much time passes. He sees injustice and works toward righteousness with a heart of love.1

It's time for me to intercede again for Gwen. We pray and for the first time I don't fight against darkness, a sensation of rejoicing releases around us. God has overcome the bitterness in her heart since we last met.

Today when I read Scripture, I focus on God's promises regarding the kingdom of heaven. We delight to hear about the place He prepares for Gwen. 2 Her eyes light up as she contemplates her time entering His Kingdom. She is jubilant. "It feels like I am getting ready to go on vacation!"

"But you don't need to pack for this."

"Or worry about what I look like in a bathing suit."

"Yeah, your heaven suit is gonna look real nice at the beach!"

She moves slow today, needing my help to walk. She cannot go more than a few steps before having to catch her breath. This indicates substantial fluid built up in her lungs.

The next time we pray I probably will need to go to her. She may never be able to return to my house.

Leroy wants her to hold him. He reaches for her and struggles against me. "I know, I know you want me to hold you, baby." She laments. I grip his wiggling frame as he gives her a gentle hug. "I want to hold you too. I wish I could. I love you, Leroy." His pudgy hand pats her back. Gwen shuts her eyes and takes in a miraculous full breath of his pure love, strengthening her for the trek to her car.

When did my walkway get this long?

No wonder Scriptures often speak of human frailty. Only days ago, Gwen literally skipped into my house, with her hands full of tarts she baked me. My generous friend, she always brings an offering: vanilla coffee, gifts for Leroy — a train, a turtle, a little book that reminded her of him. Once, she handed me an unopened box of pancake mix, wanting me to have something easy to make for breakfast. Today she is too weak to carry anything. She brought only herself — the greatest gift she ever gave me.

Day 7. Warzone.

I used to be able to go to the grocery store with my son like a normal person, make my list and march up aisle by aisle, in an attempt to fill my cart as quickly as possible. That was before God activated something in me and changed my perception.

Now when I leave this house, I am stepping into an apocalyptic warzone, a spiritual virtual reality: the world is dying around me, and I am searching for survivors. When I find someone I can help, I refuse to leave them to the unforgiving wasteland. I need to give them a map, a clue, something to help them find fresh water.

Not your ordinary errand run.

For my whole life I looked at this all wrong. I once thought when I go to the House of the Lord, to His Church, then and there, I will minister to people.

But I am the House of the Lord, where I go, there He is.[3] People are not sent to me, God sends me to them.

We know from Scripture that Jesus went about, anointed by the Holy Spirit, healing and redeeming those oppressed.[4] He is the same today as He was yesterday as He will always be.[5] Then the Holy Spirit came in His place to act as a Helper, alive within me.[6] Christ declared that those who come after Him are capable of the same, and greater works, through reliance on the Holy Spirit.[7]

No more excuses for idleness. When I go to the grocery store today, I carry the full armor of God, ready for the mission. I pull into the parking lot alongside a young woman in a small black car. The Lord shows me a giant spiderweb forming over the hood of her car, bits of earth and insects are caught inside. It's an arachnophobe's nightmare.

I jump out of my car and rush after her into the store. I do not want another burger joint fiasco on my hands. *Whatever entraps or ensnares you, may you be set free!* I will proclaim. But then she turns a corner and disappears. *Hmm.*

Then I am reminded of tremendous wisdom from my mentor. "Every time He shows you a vision," Dee said, "ask the Lord, 'Do you want me to pray or do you want me to act?' Allow Him to guide you."

This is a time, The Teacher says, **when I want you to pray.**

Because, *whoa there, Erinn, not everyone is ready to hear your craziness!*

Then as I round the coffee aisle I see a rainbow arched over the head of another girl as she dips around a corner toward the bread and crackers. I dare not tread that road — Carb Alley frightens a woman like myself who is trying to lose baby weight.

I pass her again in the safer canned food section, and the urge to speak grows strong. Tension in my chest eases when I notice her ears are covered by headphones, like somehow this excuses me from saying anything.

Tell her about the rainbow. Tell her what I have promised will to come to fruition..₈

Okay Boss let's go.

I throw several cans of green beans into my cart before making a U-turn back up the aisle. "Excuse me." I tap her elbow, hyper-aware of other shoppers. She pulls out her headphones with a smile. She has striking green eyes with gold flecks beneath dark eyelashes, maroon dyed hair. She is wearing a cool white sweatshirt with the design of paint splatters.

"This sounds crazy," I say, with a nervous bubble of laughter, "but I believe in Jesus Christ. He shows me things about people and when I looked at you I saw a rainbow. He wants you to know that what He promised you will come to fruition."

Tears fill her eyes, glistening like droplets of dew. "Thank you." Her voice is soft and her lips tremble. "Thank you. I needed to hear that today." She crosses her arms tight over her stomach, a private person, reluctant to share more.

I fumble with my purse, adjusting it on my shoulder and avoid eye contact. "It's awkward to do this, but when He speaks... Well, I thought you should know. Okay, God bless you. Have a good day!" I bob my head, then wheel the cart on to the dairy section, hoping we won't run into each other in every aisle now.

When I line up to check out, I see her leave the store. The message God gave her must have struck a chord. She hurries away, pulling her hood down to conceal her troubled face. I see the rainbow still rises above her, this time rain pours down among the misty colors.

A rainbow waits to reveal itself until a storm. So it is with my promises. The glory of their truth reveals in the trial. Jesus says.

My chest aches. *What caused such a torrential storm?* I wish I had asked her name and been more eloquent. I said *"flu-ition"* instead of *fruition,* not even knowing the word God wanted me to use. What if she needs me again? How would she find me?

Maybe I ought to print a contact card. What would such a thing say?

ERINN JOSEPHINE
BELIEVER IN THE IMPOSSIBLE
GROCERY STORE PROPHET

Hm. Sounds about right.

Good thing she needs Jesus, not me. He can meet her anywhere.

What would His calling card say?

YHWH
FATHER, SON, SPIRIT
I AM

Day 8. Expiration Date.

According to her doctors, today should be Gwen's last on Earth.

She misses our prayer session, asking me instead to pray on my own time. She can only listen or speak over the phone for a moment, "I think I am close now. My body can't keep this up much longer." She whispers between coughing fits.

Her body struggles violently to eliminate toxins in other ways now that it no longer produces urine. She vomits black slime and is unable to eat or drink anything other than sips of warm tea. Her body is swollen with fluid and feels as though it will split. Her skin, working to remove toxins too, makes her itch, a deep, all over itch, like poison ivy on the inside. No amount of scratching or medicine brings relief.

Leroy and I pray, without ceasing: *Not this way. I hate for her to go this way. Thank you, Jesus, for breaking through and overcoming her pain. Thank you for your peace over her body. Healer, Deliverer, I declare Your promises of abundant life over Gwen right now, in Jesus's name!*

Day 9. Don't Give Up, It's Just Beginning.

It is Saturday morning. I call to check on Gwen. The phone rings too many times for my comfort zone but her weary voice answers at last.

"The doctors told me I would likely die of suffocation," she says, and I hear muffled coughing. "I don't think I want to go that way."

"No! You are a child of God and with that comes benefits!" I declare, then I begin to read Psalm 103, inserting her name within the Scriptures to claim ownership over the words. "'*Gwen blesses the Lord! O her soul, and all that is within her, bless His holy name. Bless the Lord, Gwen, and forget not all His benefits. He who forgives all your iniquities; who heals all your diseases; who redeems your life from destruction; who crowns you, Gwen, with lovingkindness and tender mercies; who satisfies your mouth with good things; so that your youth, Gwen, renews like the eagle's.*'

"Gwen, in the name of Jesus, I declare you will not die of suffocation. When your appointed time comes, you enter His Kingdom with a spirit of peace not fear. You will not suffer! You will fall into a sweet sleep and awaken to the face of Jesus! '**Do not be afraid, for I am with you,**' says the Lord! Only peace and rejoicing for you in these last days! In the name of Jesus and by the power of His blood, amen!"

Gwen lives alone; she worries about dying at home unattended, but has decided against calling in hospice. "I don't want to be drugged up and unconsciousness alone with a stranger here."

"I will call you every day to check in," I promise.

"I am afraid Ethan will find me, or that my remains will be here for too long."

"If you don't answer the phone, I will come and check on you right away."

"What are you even supposed to do with a dead body?" She says with a wry chuckle.

"No idea. Sounds like something you won't have to face." This type of conversation has become my new normal. We break into laughter. Why are we laughing? Because the alternative is hopelessness and despair.

Death is ridiculous. One day you are flesh and then in the blink of an eye, separated from those who love you. It should feel more natural, this cycle of things. We are born, we live, we bring forth others to live, we die. Everyone does it. It feels unnatural because it is. Elohim, the Creator, wove us together as eternal beings. He did not create us to separate us from one another, or from Him.

Death is a product of the fall of man and a cursed world, not a product of our design. Jesus resolved this by paying the highest price. With His blood He restored our access to the Father and to the fullness of abundant everlasting life. We await the day our Lord returns to remake this world, settling this awful death thing once and for all.

A coughing fit overwhelms Gwen, she needs to rest. "I love you, sister." We say to each other.

Weeks ago, I avoided this woman. Now I consider sleeping on her living room floor out of fear that she will be gone in the blink of an eye.

No matter how much you expect death's arrival, there is no way to prepare for the moment it comes.

Part IV Scriptures

1) Hebrews 10:30 For we know him that hath said, Vengeance belongeth unto me, I will recompense, saith the Lord. And again, The Lord shall judge his people.

2) Psalm 147:3 He healeth the broken in heart, and bindeth up their wounds.

3) John 14:1-11 Let not your heart be troubled: ye believe in God, believe also in me. In my Father's house are many mansions: if it were not so, I would have told you. I go to prepare a place for you. And if I go and prepare a place for you, I will come again, and receive you unto myself; that where I am, there ye may be also. And whither I go ye know, and the way ye know. Thomas saith unto him, Lord, we know not whither thou goest; and how can we know the way? Jesus saith unto him, I am the way, the truth, and the life: no man cometh unto the Father, but by me.If ye had known me, ye should have known my Father also: and from henceforth ye know him and have seen him.Philip saith unto him, Lord, show us the Father, and it sufficeth us. Jesus saith unto him, Have I been so long time with you, and yet hast thou not known me, Philip? he that hath seen me hath seen the Father; and how sayest thou then, Show us the Father? Believest thou not that I am in the Father, and the Father in me? the words that I speak unto you I speak not of myself: but the Father that dwelleth in me, he doeth the works. Believe me that I am in the Father, and the Father in me: or else believe me for the very works' sake.

4) 1 Corinthians 3:16 Know ye not that ye are the temple of God, and that the Spirit of God dwelleth in you?

5) Acts 10:37-43 That word, I say, ye know, which was published throughout all Judaea, and began from Galilee, after the baptism which John preached; How God anointed Jesus of Nazareth with the Holy Ghost and with power: who went about doing good, and healing all that were oppressed of the devil; for God was with him. And we are witnesses of all things which he did both in the land of the Jews, and in Jerusalem; whom they slew and hanged on a tree: Him God raised up the third day, and shewed him openly; Not to all the people, but unto witnesses chosen before God, even to us, who did eat and drink with him after he rose from the dead. And he commanded us to preach unto the people, and to testify that it is he which was ordained of God to be the Judge of quick and dead. To him give all the prophets witness, that through his name whosoever believeth in him shall receive remission of sins.

6) Hebrews 13:8 Jesus Christ the same yesterday, and to day, and for ever.

7) John 14:23-27 Jesus answered and said unto him, If a man love me, he will keep my words: and my Father will love him, and we will come unto him, and make our abode with him. He that loveth me not keepeth not my sayings: and the word which

ye hear is not mine, but the Father's which sent me. These things have I spoken unto you, being yet present with you. But the Comforter, which is the Holy Ghost, whom the Father will send in my name, he shall teach you all things, and bring all things to your remembrance, whatsoever I have said unto you. Peace I leave with you, my peace I give unto you: not as the world giveth, give I unto you. Let not your heart be troubled, neither let it be afraid.

8) John 14:12 Verily, verily, I say unto you, He that believeth on me, the works that I do shall he do also; and greater works than these shall he do; because I go unto my Father.

9) Genesis 9:13 I do set my rainbow in the cloud, and it shall be for a token of a covenant between me and the earth.

Part V:

Barking Up the Wrong Tree

Day 11. Mutt Lessons

Three days have passed since Gwen was supposed to die.

I am cranky, moody, frustrated. My irritability reaches the boiling point when a troll-like howl bursts from my dog. Throughout each day, uncontrollable noise comes from this animal. To intensify the situation, our home boasts a bay window. It takes up half the wall, stretching floor to ceiling. Back in the 60s they made this window for my dog because it is her mission to perceive and acknowledge every microscopic movement in the neighborhood.

"Lexi come." I kneel on my messy kitchen floor and look her in the eyes.

Treat? Lexi asks, sitting without a command.

I shake my head. "Lexi, when an unknown human comes on the porch. When someone is hurt or needs help. If the baby makes a break for it. These times I need you to bark. When a squirrel crosses the lawn. When kids ride bikes. When the trash truck arrives — no barking." I explain with forced patience unique to a poochie mother.

Her prominent pointed ears rise when I say "bark" and she looks to the window. *Bark?* She wonders. *I think the mama-master tells me to bark?* Her attention returns, golden-brown eyes initializing Treat Hypnosis. "Nope. I'm too cranky to give out cheese today."

Don't feel sorry for Lexi; she gets plenty of snacks from the baby. And I don't think she took anything away from our talk. But who am I to judge? Because, maybe I barked up the wrong tree and overstepped my boundaries as well...

I called Gwen earlier to read Scripture and pray. Our conversation was brief. She is fighting to stay awake, to breathe. She awaits death and its tardiness exasperates her. When I get off the phone, guilt settles heavy in my gut.

Have I overstayed my welcome?

I asked for the information for her hospice center in case I need to contact them. I researched it and learned that if I find her after she passes, contacting hospice is recommended. They will set in motion final arrangements their clients have made.

Gwen was obviously uncomfortable with the question. "I will look into it myself, thanks," she said, before rushing me off the phone.

I was wrong to ask. We are close now, but I am not family. What was I thinking, asking for her private information?

Lessons like this punish me into learning when to shut my mouth. Afraid of not acting when God asks, I stagger to the opposite end of the spectrum.

Inaction's arrogant twin, Presumption. Ew.

Here is another example I don't want to share:

I recently sent an unsolicited email to my co-worker, an acquaintance.

RED FLAG #1 – No Loving Foundation. 1

Aware of the difficult position he holds and a busy season at work, I know his abilities are stretched. I decided to encourage him with some infinite wisdom.

RED FLAG #2 – Actions based on pride. 2

I sent the email to him and as a second thought, sent it separately to my boss, so she could see what I wrote.

RED FLAG #3 – No Council prior to contact. 3

I never heard back from either of them.

My boss is next on my call list. "Was my email a help or a hindrance?" I ask when I reach her.

She laughs, emitting an ironic dark chuckle. I know this well to be her sound of displeasure and never a good sign. "Yea, um, I think it came off as, what's the word? Preachy. And presumptuous. Yes, that's it. It was presumptuous."

Oh, Father in Heaven, thank you for returning me to humility.

Presumptuous and oh, the shame — preachy?

Let us commence with the wincing.

When I get off the phone with my boss, I realize I made the same mistake with Gwen. Her remaining time is precious. I assumed God placed me in charge of this when I never took the two seconds necessary to ask first. Then I further assume my friend wanted to give me access to her confidential information.

Intruder. Bike. Squirrel! Truck! I bark at the window without remembering my role. At least I know Gwen appreciates my morning check in. My focus must stay on showing her love and support in her last days, not preparing for her death.

There is a pastor Gwen has followed her entire Christian walk of 30 years. I wanted him to come to one of our prayer sessions. I have called him four times since this journey began, but I reached an answering machine each time. The voicemails I left explain Gwen's circumstances with urgency. "My neighbor Gwen has belonged to your church for decades. She is dying of renal failure. It would bless everyone if you came to see her in these last days. There is not much time left." I received no response.

I had planned to call once more and imagined surprising Gwen with the pastor's arrival, but I've howled in presumption enough for one week. I will wait to talk with Gwen about it because any visit now needs to be on her terms.

Day 12. How Much Longer?

I hesitate to admit this. I want you to think I am a good person.

The truth is I am not a good person. I am not a bad person either, but I am a person. Us persons need Jesus to help us transform into something very unlike a person.4

Having said that, here it is…

Awaiting death is exhausting. I don't want to do this anymore.

Before I call Gwen today, I almost hope she has passed. Each day that goes by winds my flesh tighter. I wait for a deadly jack-in-the-box to jump out at me. The music queued him to release days ago, but I just sit here. Watching for it. Growing more jumpy with every second.

Waiting for this to happen depletes everything within me. Gwen's anguish increases each day. I don't want her to go, but I don't want her to stay and remain sick in torment. My heart cries, *"Please God, no more suffering. May Gwen be healed or be Home. To linger here like this, that can't be the plan. Can it?"*

God told me not to come into agreement with this death. I try, but while I pray for her life, my mind has started accepting her death.

Have I failed Him?

Day 15. All Things New.

Wednesday God threw a wrench in all expectations.

Gwen is getting better.

I am astounded, then wonder, *why am I astounded?* I prayed without ceasing for this; I should be smug, not surprised.

When I call, she tells me that she is alert, peeing, eating. Talking without coughing. She takes her trash out, and went to lunch with a friend.

Thursday, she felt well enough to get angry at God. "For three years I prayed over a list of repairs to get done on my house. He never helped me. I look around at this place and it would take a freaking miracle to get the basement finished and my fence redone!"

A miracle? Can she not see the irony? Why should she care, she won't be living there anymore. Is she starting to think about a future?

"A miracle!" Says the woman who should have died or at least be comatose, doped in waves of morphine by hospice. The woman who should be unable to draw enough breath to yell.

I shake my head. A few days ago, she struggled to draw breath enough for a 'Hello'. Now she rants for ten minutes about home repairs.

Friday. Seven days after Gwen's projected death date.

She wakes at 5:30 a.m., encountering Holy Spirit all around her. Her own spirit fills with song and praise. She puts worship music on, enjoys a refreshing shower, and makes Leroy and I a fancy lunch.

I kid you not — the woman brings us lunch!

The last time she came here, she fought to climb the steps. Now she calls to me from her car, "Hey, can Leroy have a soda? I brought some sodas!" Her arms are fill with a pot of creamy shrimp penne, and a bag hangs from her shoulder with snacks.

I keep a poker face as I greet her, "It's pronounced 'Pop' at this house," I tease. "But yeah, he can have some if you let me carry it."

She skips up the steps. Not letting me carry the *pop*.

I no longer contain my surprise when she lifts my thirty-pound child and serves a plate for him while he balances on her hip. "Aren't you supposed to be dying?"

"Right? I told Jesus yesterday I am starting to get offended! Nothing to 'ooh and ahh' about. It's only a week past my death date."

I am oohing and ahhing. 70% Oohing. 30% Ahhing. 100 Billion% Praising!

Gwen says if her health continues to improve, she will get more bloodwork done in the spring. "Maybe the problem was never my kidneys in the first place."

I study the healthy color in her face and the strength she moves with, remembering the woman who inched down my walkway last visit. This is not that woman, but I am skeptical. "Possible. But you should go in for bloodwork right away. I am curious to know what's happening in your body now, compared to your initial diagnosis."

Leroy climbs into Gwen's lap. He grabs her face, forcing her eyes on him, and murmurs baby words just for her. Anytime she turns her head to speak to me, he pushes her chin back, making it clear who this visit is about. In toddler years, hundreds of days have passed since Leroy saw his dear friend. Last time she left so sick. He must have known.

I couldn't get him to eat anything this morning, now he devours Gwen's feast. Her grandmother heart delights in feeding him applesauce as he sits in her lap. After thanking her with apple-saucy kisses, Leroy jumps down to conduct a performance on his slide for his biggest fans. He slides down, lands on his feet, and leaps up into a stomping dance. We laugh and applaud over and over. *'A merry heart doeth good like a medicine.'*5 and Leroy is powerful medicine indeed.

Once Leroy settles down for a nap, Gwen says, "It occurred to me yesterday, that awful dialysis center may still charge Medicare for my attendance even though I stopped going. I don't have any proof, but it felt like a word from God."

I think it might be important to reveal the icky-ness of the center. "Considering what you've told me about the place, I would not be surprised. Have you thought about contacting Medicare to confirm?"

Gwen waves the idea off, "I guess I could. But whatever goes on there, God will expose the truth."

Yes, God exposes truth but what about faith with action? I wonder. *Not every battle is yours to fight, my child.* The Lord tells me with a gentle conviction unique to His Spirit. *Thank you, Lord, I don't want them all.* I let the subject drop. Too many great things are happening to meditate on the bad.

Not only do I see a profound change in Gwen's spirit, she even looks different. She cut her own hair.

This is significant. I just know it! Someone else close to me had a similar experience.

My mom has struggled against a painful auto-immune disease for 25 years. She suffered an especially bleak season last year. Not only was she existing in a state of chronic pain, her spirit was stumbling through bitterness and spiritual separation. These plagues ripped Christ's promise of abundant life7 from her memory.

After Christmas she grew exhausted by the gap between her and her First Love.8 "Jesus, I miss my friend." Her heart cried.

A couple days later while experiencing another rough morning of physical and spiritual pain, the Spirit of the Lord spoke to my mom. ***Get up. Go to the bathroom. Start cutting your hair and do not stop until I tell you.***

In obedience, but feeling a bit silly, Mama began to snip away her shoulder-length hair. She stopped when all that remained were little curls in an adorable bob. She left the bathroom awakened from her darkness, the pain of her heart also cut away by His loving hands. Mom laughed at the absurdity of it as she tried to explain to me what happened. She didn't need to explain; I saw the changes in her after Jesus brought her back to His heart.9

God speaks in weird ways. At the time, mom and I reasoned that He used this hair cutting as a test of obedience to His voice. Which was probably true, however today, I decided maybe there was another reason...

When I noticed that Gwen had chopped her thick locks. I commented on how nice it looks.

She ran her fingers through the strands and smiled, "I grew tired of it getting in my way. So, I took some scissors to it."

"You cut it yourself?" I say, mom's experience tickling my memory.

"Yea. It feels a lot better."

Huh. What are you up to God?

Now I got to know about this hair cutting thing. After Gwen leaves I call mom to get her on it. Her degree in journalism makes her the best researcher I know. She calls right back.

Behold! She found it in Leviticus 14:8 *He who is to be cleansed shall wash his clothes, shave off all his hair, and wash himself in water, that he may be clean.* God required this of the Israelites as part of the cleansing ritual after being healed of leprosy.

The shaved head marked healing.

Mighty God declares Gwen cleansed of the darkness once afflicting her spirit, using my mother's testimony as a precedent!

Part V Scriptures

1) Romans 12:9 Let love be without dissimulation. Abhor that which is evil; cleave to that which is good.

2) Proverbs 16:18 Pride goeth before destruction, and a haughty spirit before a fall.

3) Proverbs 12:15 The way of a fool is right in his own eyes: but he that hearkeneth unto counsel is wise.

4) 2 Corinthians 5:17 Therefore if any man be in Christ, he is a new creature: old things are passed away; behold, all things are become new.

5) Proverbs 17:22 A merry heart doeth good like a medicine: but a broken spirit drieth the bones.

6) James 2:15-17 If a brother or sister be naked, and destitute of daily food, And one of you say unto them, Depart in peace, be ye warmed and filled; notwithstanding ye give them not those things which are needful to the body; what doth it profit? Even so faith, if it hath not works, is dead, being alone.

7) John 10:10 The thief cometh not, but for to steal, and to kill, and to destroy: I am come that they might have life, and that they might have it more abundantly.

8) Revelations 2:4 Nevertheless I have somewhat against thee, because thou hast left thy first love.

9) Isaiah 40:10-11 Behold, the Lord God will come with strong hand, and his arm shall rule for him: behold, his reward is with him, and his work before him. He shall feed his flock like a shepherd: he shall gather the lambs with his arm, and carry them close to his heart, and shall gently lead those that are with young.

10) Isaiah 55:8-9 For my thoughts are not your thoughts, neither are your ways my ways, saith the Lord. For as the heavens are higher than the earth, so are my ways higher than your ways, and my thoughts than your thoughts.

Part VI:

Revelations

Ethan took Gwen to church on Sunday and praise, *praise*, – Pastor Tim and his wife, Annie, prayed over her after the service.

"I'm so glad they spent time with you. I tried to invite them to a prayer session. I left a few messages. Did they say anything about it?" I ask.

"No, they didn't mention it. Maybe the messages never went through," Gwen said. "Listen to this, a few years back Tim received dialysis for acute kidney failure. When he underwent treatment, he hated the clinics so much he tried several before finding one he was comfortable in. Awful places. I hope kidney failure becomes extinct and drives them out of business."

"Amen! What was their take on your situation?"

"Annie tried to talk me into dialysis again. I don't think she was listening. Tim seemed to get it though. He wanted to know my timeframe."

"What did he think when you told him you are 12 days past your timeframe?"

"I'm not sure. We prayed for God's will to be done."

I heard a lot about "God's will" growing up as a Christian in America. As if no matter what happens, it is God's will and we should accept it as it is. If that were true, why would Jesus tell us to pray "Thy will be Done on Earth as it is In Heaven."? [1]

Why pray this if His will already cancels out every other will floating around? Is that what wills do? Kinda just float around?

How can we know the will of God? Our biggest hope rests in Jesus, who did not act apart from the will of Father God. [2] Intimacy with the Holy Spirit and quality time within God's Holy Word provide a clearer map as well. If you are willing to listen to His voice, even if it opposes what you want, then you are freed to follow the path He set for you. Sometimes He drops bread crumbs and other times boulders.

Still, many questions remain about God's will. If we had the answers, we would be God.

Whew, not my job!

But I ponder on it because of what it means for Gwen. While many voices fill her ears about what needs to happen, the one that matters is God's. He can speak through others, like Annie and Tim, Ethan and Gwen's family members. [3] However it will be up to the Holy Spirit to convince Gwen's heart.

I realize now why He asked me to only pray Scriptures over her. Gwen gets a lot of opinions, she never needed mine.

Can I tell you what I want to happen? If I were making the choices here...

Gwen would live long enough to witness the redemption of her son and see the truth revealed about the dialysis centers. All darkness in her life would be destroyed at the foot of the cross.

And Gwen's body would be physically healed.

"Gwen, in the name of Jesus, I pray that the voice of the Living God will rise over all others as a mighty roar within you. May you follow Him and Him alone," I pray, keeping my hopes quiet.

"Amen." We say together.

Day 18. Exposed to the Elements.

I dream of walking naked in my backyard during late autumn.

I head into the house from the fence line and glimpse my next-door neighbors watching through cracks in their enclosed patio.

"They have probably seen me naked before," I think, unashamed.

I stroll into my house through the open backdoor. Dismay overwhelms me when I notice the plants dying in the backroom. Their once vibrant flowers browned and wilting because I left the door open. The cold air damaged their sensitive petals.

I assure you, I make no habit of walking around naked in my backyard.

As soon as I'm fully awake, I look up symbols from this dream in a Christian interpretation book, but my spirit rejects what I find. The book references nakedness as unashamed preaching of the gospel, quoting the Scripture "clothed in glory."4

No. That's not right. What am I missing?

My entire life I've had elaborate, vivid dreams. After extensive study on them, I am convinced most are spiritual in nature and fall into three categories:

104

<u>Conversation:</u> *The spirit reaches out to God* using images and scattered thoughts with a desire for understanding. He replies with His own images and clarifications.

<u>Infiltration:</u> *From the enemy.* These dreams are woven to misdirect, confuse, frighten, or tempt.

<u>Word from God:</u> *We awaken knowing their significance.* As we sleep, we encounter the Living God and the powerful sense of Him lingers with the rise of the sun. These dreams encourage or comfort. They give insight into the truth of a matter, warn about physical or spiritual danger, and can be answers to our prayerful questions.

When I strive to interpret my own dreams, my brain often knots and stumbles. Frustration further builds when I depend only on the tools given to me (e.g., guides and research) rather than Scripture and the Creator of those tools.

"Maybe you should seek out His Spirit first, before going to your books." I was recently counseled by a Christ-brother on my prayer team.

That should have been obvious. Yet, I dive so deep into God's mystery I can forget His simplicity, then wonder why I hit a roadblock trying to obtain this gift.

Obtain a gift? Is not a gift, given? His voice tests me.

Lights go on. *Of course, Father. A gift is not forced, learned, or developed. A gift is Given.*

105

True Dream Interpretation is reliant on the Holy Spirit. Some great books are out there that help guide the believer through the symbolism in God's word. But who else translates a word from God but the Holy One Himself? And in the intimacy of a dream, God speaks directly to each child, not the author of a dream book. What "cold" means to me might mean something different to another.

When I consider nakedness outside in the cold, the word "exposed" forms.

Quiet, I listen for His voice. The symbols congeal, a blurred idea, like a memory drawn forth from a smell. If I chase it, I lose understanding. If I turn my focus to Jesus, allowing the thoughts to come to me, the message takes shape.

The enemy sees you, and your exposed weaknesses. Be vigilant, an open door endangers your spirit's growth, He warns.

Where in my life are "open doors?"

The back door.

A part of my life less noticeable? Easier for me to neglect? Neither of those click. *Will you show me, Lord?*

He falls silent.

I meditate on His warning and a strategy forms.

I need to be watchful in prayer and honest with Him, studying and meditating on His word more. It would be wise to take time blessing my home, something I did when moving in. I will again anoint all the entry ways with oil and walk the boundary lines of my yard while listening to worship music and praying in the Spirit.₅ I will ask my brothers and sisters in Christ to pray for protection over me and my household.

Day 22. The Fishing Net

Friday, Leroy and I go to Gwen's house to borrow a saw for some pre-spring cleanup. She strains to breathe again and has episodes of fatigue. "I am so ready to go," she gasps.

Is she? Then why is she still here?

We stay for tea. I chase Leroy as he tests every remote-control in Gwen's house. We listen to worship music and the songs she has chosen for her funeral service. When she spoke with Pastor Tim, she confirmed that he would do her service. She decided she wants him to tell the story of Jesus asking the disciples to cast their net out once more.

"This story is like my memorial service," Gwen says. "You are the only one who will be there who believes in Jesus. When Tim speaks, he will be casting my fishing net out one more time over my family and friends."

My body covers with goose bumps, my eyes fill with tears, as we discuss the story in Scripture.

Peter said to the other disciples, "I am going fishing."

"We will go with you," they said, but that night they caught nothing.

At day break, Jesus stood on the shore; yet the disciples did not know Him. Jesus called to them, *"Children, do you have any fish?"*

"No." They replied, still not recognizing it was the Lord.

Jesus said to them, *"Cast the net once more on the right side of the boat, and you will find some."*

So, they cast it, and now they were unable to haul it in because of the quantity of fish.

"It is the Lord!" John cried out.

When Peter heard that, he threw himself into the sea and swam to shore to greet Jesus. The other disciples came by boat, dragging the net full of fish.

Once on land, they saw a charcoal fire in place, with fish laid out on it, and bread. Jesus said to them, *"Bring some of the fish you just caught."*

So, Peter went aboard and hauled the net ashore, full of 153 large fish. And although there were so many, the net was untorn. Jesus said to them, *"Come and have breakfast."*

Now none of the disciples dared ask Him, "Who are you?" They knew it was the Lord.

Jesus came and took the bread and gave it to them, and so with the fish.

This was now the third time that Jesus was revealed to the disciples after He was raised from the dead. (John 21:2-14 Erinn's Version)

Maybe she needs to cast the net out again, not Pastor Tim. Maybe she needs to give this life-thing one more try.

We have brought her a page out of my coloring book. (Yes, *my* coloring book. Not Leroy's. A lot of adults do it so, minimal smirking, please. And besides, the entire time I colored this page I thought, *Gwen would like this.*) I colored it like a rainbow. Hidden within a spray of hearts and flowers is a dove. Leroy colored on the back and we wrote a message of love on it. Gwen displays the "work of art" between a family photo and a vase filled with tulips from her best friend, Bailey, who brings fresh flowers every time she visits.

"My favorite picture of Ethan from when he was a kid," Gwen says, when I pick up the picture of a grinning Ethan standing with a bike. "One of my favorite days with him, too. It was the day he learned to ride a bike. As a single mom, there are some things that come harder than others. Boys need a good man in their life. Him and I worked at riding that dang bike for so long. We couldn't get it. I was dating a nice guy at the time who came by. He took Ethan down the block, said three words to him and then sent him on his way. He started riding along like he'd been doing it forever! He was so proud. You can see it in the picture," she smiles, then winces at the fluid that has built up in her legs.

I lay my hands on her and we pray. "Thank you, Lord, that Gwen stays here until Your appointed time. Thank you, Jesus, for a peaceful, painless passing. When Gwen enters Your Kingdom, she leaves this earth as a woman healed by the blood of her Savior. For Your Glory and by the power of the name of Jesus..."

I hope Gwen gets it soon…how loved and needed she is. Love draws us into life. Does she resist its pull because she set her mind on death?

Part VI Scriptures

1) Luke 11:1-4 And it came to pass, that, as he was praying in a certain place, when he ceased, one of his disciples said unto him, Lord, teach us to pray, as John also taught his disciples. And he said unto them, When ye pray, say, Our Father which art in heaven, Hallowed be thy name. Thy kingdom come. Thy will be done, as in heaven, so in earth. Give us day by day our daily bread. And forgive us our sins; for we also forgive every one that is indebted to us. And lead us not into temptation; but deliver us from evil.

2) John 12:49 For I have not spoken of myself; but the Father which sent me, he gave me a commandment, what I should say, and what I should speak.

3) James 3:13 Who is a wise man and endued with knowledge among you? let him shew out of a good conversation his works with meekness of wisdom.

4) 2 Corinthians 5:2-5 For in this we groan, earnestly desiring to be clothed upon with our house which is from heaven: If so be that being clothed we shall not be found naked. For we that are in this tabernacle do groan, being burdened: not for that we would be unclothed, but clothed upon, that mortality might be swallowed up of life.

5) Ephesians 6:18 Praying always with all prayer and supplication in the Spirit and watching thereunto with all perseverance and supplication for all saints.

Part VII:

The Plane Didn't Crash

Day 24. Time Cannot Govern Its Creator.

Today is a great American holiday, the Super Bowl.

The grocery store is a mess of humanity and produce, everyone in a hurry to get the ripest avocados and six-packs of cheap beer.

An elegant woman draws my spirit's attention. The female embodiment of the American Dream, her clothes speak of success and her face is kind with smiling eyes. But when I look at her I see a knife through her back into her heart.

Someone you deeply love betrayed you. My spirit says to hers as I pray and add bananas to my cart. I feel Jesus easing the knife out, it dissolves in His grasp. He encases this lovely lady's heart in His scarred hands and restores the wound to new flesh.

"He works to restore your relationship with this person. Don't give up," I want to say. If I were her, I would want to know this good news. But God's Spirit holds me back from speaking, so I respect His perfect timing and remain silent. For now, I praise Him for the promise over her healing and move on.

At the checkout counter, a nine-year-old girl dances beside her mother. A yellow headband with a bow attempts to tame long curling brown hair.

I am disturbed. Visions usually come like a waking dream, a dream-world layered over reality. But, this time is different. The scene draws me in as an observer, the grocery store disappearing from sight.

This girl is now 16-18 years old. She walks along a dark city street at night and I follow. She pays no attention to her surroundings, focusing on her phone. She wears a dark brown leather jacket over a short blue-flowered dress. A cold breeze lifts her long curly hair. She approaches a street lamp and it flickers.

A flickering light is never a good sign.

The Lord takes me ahead of her and shows me someone concealed in the dark alcove of a brick building. The alcove is wide enough to fit two large men shoulder-to-shoulder and deep enough to conceal a person. A human predator waiting for prey is huddled in the building's shadows.

I return to the grocery store blinking in surprise. This little girl, once again safe and laughing with her mother, comes back into focus, her yellow bow slipping from wild hair. She reaches for some snacks from the grocery bag.

That was a vision of future events, not symbolic. I wish I could explain how I know this, but it is knowledge apart from sense. I am in a mama bear rage. *NO!* I utter a war cry within. *This girl will not be harmed! What do I do, Lord?*

Pray. Pray for a policeman to drive up and offer her a ride. Pray for angels to surround her. Pray for interference.

116

I prayed with all the fight in my heart, and I continue to pray whenever I think of it. God resides outside of time. He is mighty to save.[1] He goes before this girl, and I trust He will deliver her from this evil. My job is not to answer the "how?" and the "why?" My job is not to make sense to you. Jesus calls me, not to reason, but to obedience.

He told me to pray against the harm of this sweet innocent child. Please, pray with me, together, let us declare Psalm 91[2] over this moment.

Maybe one day, when we are in Glory, He will show us the fruit of this prayer.

Day 25. Everything Changes.

I dream I am standing in my parent's backyard with my mother. It is dusk. Shocked, we see a strange aircraft falling from the sky. I reach my hands out and pray. "Thank You, Jesus! Thank You, You will not allow this plane to crash on anyone's house!"

The plane lifts back up.

The craft now hovers above the tree line to a neighborhood on our right. As it passes over us, we see missiles attached on each side, white and red in color. We watch it land a few streets away.

Night falls. With foreboding, my family and our neighbors collect in the front yard. We scramble to get children into the arms of their mothers.

People from the area where the aircraft landed come toward us. Soundless, they move through an unpaved alleyway connecting our street to theirs. They step with the silent precision of soldiers on enemy territory.

They are men, women, and children who evacuated the neighborhood undetected as soon as the craft landed. Their grim expressions confirm it; this is an invasion. Enemies are among us.

A collective unspoken decision is made among us. We prepared for this, expected an attack. Without a sound my husband hands my brother a large firearm. The other men pass around weapons and pull on tactical gear.

118

Women and children move with efficiency. I stand among them, my son in my arms. The men surround us in an arc, facing the alleyway, weapons drawn and pointing to the mouth of the alley. When the invaders come, they will walk right into our ambush. We wait with fierce expectation.

I awake, glad to find it is a typical Monday morning. The importance of the dream clings like fog as I pursue my normal routine.

I call Gwen for our prayer session. Gusting wind blows through the background as she speaks. "I only have a few minutes. Bailey is driving me to the hospital right now."

"Everything okay? Are you getting testing done?"

"No, actually...Erinn, I decided to get back on dialysis. A chair opened for me at this hospital where I wanted to go from the beginning. They were full until now."

Two days ago, she showed me her funeral music and we went over her plans for the memorial service. Is this sudden change of heart real? "Gwen! Wow, that's great news! What changed?"

"Of course, Bailey and Ethan have been trying to talk me into this ever since I went off the treatment. Then Pastor Tim's sermon on Sunday opened my eyes. Yesterday I decided to get back on dialysis, and today they called to tell me a chair opened up."

Is this over? Did we win?

"The enemy thought he had me. He almost did." She says. "Will you tell Leroy?"

Still reeling, I call for my son. "Bubbies, Gwen decided to live!" Leroy seizes the phone, and murmurs into it as he rushes away. I hear Gwen crooning to him as I pry the device from his iron toddler fist. "Gwen? Gwen, I'm back. Leroy got ahold of the phone."

"That's all right, I wanted to talk to him. Hey, I have to go, we are pulling into the parking lot right now."

But I have a thousand more questions! "Okay, this is just wonderful news! Have a great appointment. Love you!"

This woman wanted death and now chose life. Halleluiah!

Halleluiah! Jesus, I want Gwen fully healed and alive for many years to come. I want a miraculous set of perfect kidneys in her body. Thank You, God, for the wonders that occurred, for this chair that opened for her and for keeping her alive when off of dialysis. Thank You for allowing me a part in Your work here. Halleluiah!

But wait...Was that it? Is this over? Did I miss something?

Maybe it is just anti-climactic. Maybe I expected a movie kind of ending. Gwen and I take down bad guys at a corrupted dialysis clinic. As the police drags them away, sparkling rain falls from heaven. It heals everyone in the clinic, including Gwen, and we all rush out just before the building explodes! Happily Ever After.

Insane, I know.

God does go big when it's appropriate. After all, He parted the seas, freed the Israelites from the Egyptians, came into this world under a celestial miracle, then three days after a gruesome death, shocked the world forever by shattering His gravestone and showing back up.

I believe all these unbelievable enormous miracles. However, His movements in our lives are usually gentler, like a light touch when sleeping. If distracted, we are in danger of missing out on hearing the still small voice of the Creator. 3

He parted the seas, but the promised land wasn't located directly on the other side. The Israelites were forced to trust God on His promises as they continued onward. They lost sight of these promises and wandered aimlessly for years. And yes, the story of Jesus' birth is one filled with the drama of miracles, yet nothing much happened for the next couple decades.

Imagine the shock of His death after three years of a miraculous ministry. Poor confused disciples: *"So that's it then? Yea, everyone He touched is healed. He walked on water and multiplied a ton of food. Does it even matter? He's dead now. It's over."*

It wasn't over.

In the end of the sabbath, as it began to dawn toward the first day of the week, came Mary Magdalene and the other Mary to see the tomb.

121

And, behold, a great earthquake: for the angel of the Lord descended from heaven, and came and rolled back the stone from the door, and sat upon it.

His countenance like lightning, and his raiment white as snow: And for fear of him the guards did shake and became as dead men.

And the angel answered and said unto the women, 'Fear not ye: for I know that ye seek Jesus, which was crucified. He is not here: for He is risen, as He said. Come, see the place where the Lord lay."

And go quickly and tell His disciples that He is risen from the dead; and, behold, He goeth before you into Galilee; there shall ye see Him: lo, I have told you.' Matthew 28:1-7 KJV

Gwen's tomb is still empty, now the real work begins.

"Therefore, choose life so you and your descendants may live."4

We cannot comprehend the outpouring of blessings this decision released over Gwen, Ethan, and her grandson. Her descendants. Gwen's choice freed a lifetime of blessings.

Not to say everything comes easy now. Walking the right path never meant a road clear of debris. Our Father will ask us to step out in faith. We need to continue seeking His word and declaring it in the hardest moments as well as the joyful ones.

Day 25. We Will Be Ready.

I drive home from my prayer team meeting.

The highway quiets in the late hour, the city lights reflecting off the fresh pavement of the street. In my rearview mirror I check on the baby, his head drops to the side until he stops fighting the pull of sleep. *What did my dream mean last night Lord?* I pray, the power of it still gripping my spirit.

Tell me everything you remember. Relive it. See the details.

I stand in my parent's backyard with my mother.

Mother represents my bride, the Church. Your childhood home is your family.

We look up and see an aircraft falling from the sky. I begin praying. The plane lifts back up and flies over us. There are missiles on each side.

An armed enemy, unwelcome.

It lands a few streets away. Everyone gathers. We know this is an invasion, but we are not surprised.
The Church gathers against a known threat.

My husband hands my brother a firearm. The other men pass around weapons and pull on tactical gear. The men surround women and children with their weapons drawn toward the alley.

*I am the husband. The Church puts on the armor of God.*₅

We know the invaders come. We wait for them.

Truly I say to you my child, your prayers foil the plans of the enemy. I conceal My innerworkings from him as he prepares an assault on My people.

*The enemy prowls as a lion expecting victims to devour,*₆ *instead he is ambushed by well-equipped soldiers prepared for victory.*

Part VII Scriptures

1) Zephaniah 3:17 The Lord thy God in the midst of thee is mighty; he will save, he will rejoice over thee with joy; he will rest in his love, he will joy over thee with singing.

2) Psalm 91 He that dwelleth in the secret place of the most High shall abide under the shadow of the Almighty. I will say of the Lord, He is my refuge and my fortress: my God; in him will I trust. Surely he shall deliver thee from the snare of the fowler, and from the noisome pestilence. He shall cover thee with his feathers, and under his wings shalt thou trust: his truth shall be thy shield and buckler. Thou shalt not be afraid for the terror by night; nor for the arrow that flieth by day; Nor for the pestilence that walketh in darkness; nor for the destruction that wasteth at noonday. A thousand shall fall at thy side, and ten thousand at thy right hand; but it shall not come nigh thee. Only with thine eyes shalt thou behold and see the reward of the wicked. Because thou hast made the Lord, which is my refuge, even the most High, thy habitation; There shall no evil befall thee, neither shall any plague come nigh thy dwelling. For he shall give his angels charge over thee, to keep thee in all thy ways. They shall bear thee up in their hands, lest thou dash thy foot against a stone. Thou shalt tread upon the lion and adder: the young lion and the dragon shalt thou trample under feet. Because he hath set his love upon me, therefore will I deliver him: I will set him on high, because he hath known my name. He shall call upon me, and I will answer him: I will be with him in trouble; I

will deliver him, and honour him. With long life will I satisfy him and shew him my salvation.

3) 1 Kings 19:11-12 And he said, Go forth, and stand upon the mount before the Lord. And, behold, the Lord passed by, and a great and strong wind rent the mountains, and brake in pieces the rocks before the Lord; but the Lord was not in the wind: and after the wind an earthquake; but the Lord was not in the earthquake: And after the earthquake a fire; but the Lord was not in the fire: and after the fire a still small voice.

4) Deuteronomy 30:19 I call heaven and earth to record this day against you, that I have set before you life and death, blessing and cursing: therefore choose life, that both thou and thy seed may live.

5) Ephesians 6:10-18 Finally, my brethren, be strong in the Lord, and in the power of his might. Put on the whole armour of God, that ye may be able to stand against the wiles of the devil. For we wrestle not against flesh and blood, but against principalities, against powers, against the rulers of the darkness of this world, against spiritual wickedness in high places. Wherefore take unto you the whole armour of God, that ye may be able to withstand in the evil day, and having done all, to stand. Stand therefore, having your loins girt about with truth, and having on the breastplate of righteousness; And your feet shod with the preparation of the gospel of peace; Above all, taking the shield of faith, wherewith ye

shall be able to quench all the fiery darts of the wicked. And take the helmet of salvation, and the sword of the Spirit, which is the word of God: Praying always with all prayer and supplication in the Spirit and watching thereunto with all perseverance and supplication for all saints.

6) 1 Peter 5:8 Be sober, be vigilant; because your adversary the devil, as a roaring lion, walketh about, seeking whom he may devour.

Part VIII:

A Reclaimed Destiny

Gwen is back to three days a week on dialysis, at my kitchen table she recounts the sermon that changed everything.

"Pastor Tim spoke on Nehemiah returning to Jerusalem to rebuild the walls and the way enemy nations opposed it.₁ This story is like spiritual warfare. The opposing nations reacted with mockery because they said, 'Even if they somehow get it done, the wall would be so weak an animal could knock it down and all their efforts would be in vain.' Which in our language is, 'Why try? You aren't going to make it. Even if you do, you'll fail eventually. Give up.'

"But Nehemiah responded to this by praying to the Lord to fight for him and setting guards on the walls. That way the men never left an opening for the assault, they altered between guarding and building until they completed the wall. Tim said, 'Building and battling are part of Christian life. Keep working until the wall is finished.'

"And suddenly my eyes opened to the lies I believed about my death." Gwen starts to cry as she tells me about Ethan, and the struggles he faces keeping his family together. "I believed if I died I could get him in the house and it would fix the brokenness in his family. I was willing to die to give him what he needed." She laughs through her tears, shaking her head and grabbing a tissue from my hand. "Now I realize that made no sense."

What a backwards twisted up, double knotted lie she was fed. How quickly these ideas tangled her heart and mind and warped her into believing an early death might improve rather than devastate the life of her child. Yes, Ethan will inherit some things, but how could that heal the hurt of a broken home?

Here enters the Lord Jesus, crowned in glory. Patient, He works out the tangles of this lie until He frees Gwen.

I marvel at God's work. I expected this woman to die but life won over death. "Would you like me to bring you to a Monday night prayer meeting? We can start focusing on praying for you to be healed."

"I feel content with my sickness, I am okay with it not changing because I still look forward to going Home. I want to be with Jesus. But now I don't want to show up to that party too early." Gwen says.

This reminds me of a story about Jesus as He walked a dusty road on a clear morning…

I can see it now:

"Jesus! Jesus of Nazareth!" Excitement in the crowds on the road grows.

A blind man begging by the roadside hears the shouting and his heart leaps into his throat. Jesus. THE Jesus?

132

He feels a man walking close and reaches out, "What is this? Why are they shouting?"

"It is Jesus of Nazareth, He is coming this way." The others confirm.

The chaos increases, and the blind man knows the Lord must be drawing nearer. Will his voice be heard above this crowd?

"Jesus! Son of David! Have mercy on me!" He cries out.

Only the noise of the crowd answers.

"Jesus! Jesus! Son of David, have mercy on me!" He screams the words with all the strength in his lungs.

"Hush, man. You embarrass yourself." Someone close by rebukes him. He can hear the others laughing, but soon their reprimands are drowned by his own shouting. "Son of David! Son of David! Have mercy on me! Have mercy!"

The air changes, as though he now stands in the shade of a great tree by a spring.

He heard. He came.

"What do you want me to do for you?" says the soft and mighty voice of Immanuel. (Luke 18:35-40 Erinn's Version)

The blind man asked for his eyesight to be healed. But Gwen's response to this question was different, "Heal my soul," she asked, because for her the true suffering was not of the body but of the heart.

I won't give up praying for her to experience a miracle in her body, but out of respect for Gwen's decision I will not press the matter. Because the greatest miracle promised to us is the one we carry through the gift of eternal life by the blood of Jesus Christ.

He prepares a place for us, His Heavenly Kingdom lit by His Glory. We will rejoice together in a place where death, pain, sickness, and grief are nonexistent! When her time comes, Gwen will awaken to the smiling face of Jesus and hear His glorious voice say, **You fought the fight. You finished the race. Well done good and faithful servant.** 2 The saints and angels of heaven will rejoice, "She is home! She comes to us victorious!"

I mediate on the question Ethan posed when we met last month.

"What kind of Father asks his child to stay harvesting in the field when their hands bleed. When they cry, and beg to come inside? What kind of Father treats his child like that?"

I could not answer then, but now I see the truth played out before my eyes — Death is not necessary to rest within His Kingdom. Jesus leads us beside quiet waters. Holy Spirit, our Perfect Helper, brings the Kingdom to us. The love of faithful Father God surrounds us. We enjoy seasons of rest and respite from harvesting. In these seasons He draws us nearer to His heart reviving, restoring, and making us new. He refills the heart with joy, energy, and excitement for the sunrise.

*"Our youth is renewed like an eagle's."*₃

Are you weary? Have you yet to see restoration?

Ask someone to read Scripture over you. Listen to worship music and dance. Turn off bad news and watch something that makes you laugh. Treat your body like the temple it is.

Should the eyes of a temple focus on your friend's social media page for hours? Should the mouth of your temple eat foods causing sickness? The ears of your temple listen to bad news reports or gossip?

"Taste and see that the Lord is good."₄ Use your mouth for praise, speaking positive words of life. Allow someone to see your hurting. Humble yourself and ask for prayer. Hear wise council and encouragement from your brothers and sisters.

Still not restored? There are seasons of dormancy, but seasons end. You will awaken to the sound of birds singing in the spring. Listen. Listen for His quiet voice. Cut your hair or go for a walk in the mountains.

Reach. You may not see it yet, but the Lord reaches for you right now, ready to care for you.

Some nights Leroy wakes crying in the dark. There is no nightlight in his room, no need. I know where he is. I awake to the sound of him calling. When I come to him, his eyes are closed, and his hands reach for me. He does not need to see me reaching for him, he knows his mother will comfort him.

Don't give up. Take a break in His arms for a few minutes. A day. Years. He knows what you need to be healed of before He sends you back out into the race.

Rest in the shade of His love and hear His voice.

What do you want Me to do for you?

Day 32. What the Lord Has Done.

Snow fog settles over everything. Days like this draw me under the covers and it seems unnatural to get up. How did this change transpire in just over a month?

I think of the person Gwen was when the year began. She met each day with bitterness and negativity. Now she smiles without effort, laughs often, and no longer refers to her circumstances with self-pity or anger. It is pleasant to be in her company; the words she speaks bless those around her.

I want to accept responsibility for the change. I want to wrap myself in the glory of it and say, *What a perfect friend I am. Look what I accomplished!* Oh, come on, Ego my involvement was limited. I showed her love in the form of my time and energy. I shared the joy of my child. Yet I would not have any of these things if my Father had not given them. When I committed these gifts back to Him, *Come,* He said, *Be a voice crying out in the wilderness.₅ Speak My words and watch the fruit ripen.*

God said I would be a vessel. "A vessel of what?" I asked. Then Leroy and I became vessels for an outpouring of His Love.

Have I changed as well?

The Holy Spirit has not shown me visions in public for days. Like an addict I hunger for more and am disappointed when nothing happens. But rest is important, because He is addictive.

I imagine the disciples at the end of a long day. They sit around a fire. Some stargaze, lying on a thin woven mat, dirty hands resting on unimpressive, weather beaten chests. Others stare at empty wooden bowls, crumbs dangling from their beards.

The One, Jesus of Nazareth, eats His fish in calm silence, waiting for His followers to explode with questions. No questions tonight. Everyone's eyes glaze over, their fragmented thoughts dancing because today a girl, once dead, came back to life. *"Talitha...arise"* they can still hear Him say in a mighty voice like rushing water.

I must be different.

Worldly things I once enjoyed, seem cheap now. My flesh weakens, and my spirit grows stronger. I don't mean to sound pious. I can take as much credit for my own changes as I can for Gwen's. You can't give a child a piece of steak if he is unable to chew. The Lord waited for me to grow before feeding me heartier meats.[6]

Growth should not be confused with perfection. If anything, my imperfections rise to the surface like a blister. *Ew.* I know. But you need to understand how icky this is. There is no growth without resistance. My flesh stresses out, recoiling at the deprivation of its desires.

It manifests as becoming a contentious wife. My husband, Tylor, is bewildered time and again as I fight with him on simple, silly things. I want to make amends but everything he says offends me. He called my defensive response "aggressive."

I didn't think I had an aggressive bone in my body. Poor Ty. I laid my head on his shoulder and told him how much I love him. "You are a good husband and a brilliant father. I have no ground to accuse you."

I remember what Gwen told me about Pastor Tim's sermon, "Building and battling are part of Christian life." Gwen isn't the only one called to do some building now. I have walls of my own needing repairs.

Day 34. Wake Up, We're Marching Out.

Hey…Are you awake?

Hey, wake up.

I must divert from my story of Gwen because something happened again, it is time for you to take up your armor. Polish your shield. Sharpen your sword.

Another school shooting, 17 more of our young people taken.

Are you awake yet? *Wake up!*

God's people are everywhere. In every neighborhood, every school, in night clubs and at concerts. In every nation and every tongue there is one of you.

Seventeen more kids stolen and countless dropping like flies in winter. Victims of suicide, drugs, inner city violence and immeasurable other cancers of a cursed and dying world.

Wake up. You can change this.

YOU!

Time for a revolution. Time to take our land back.

You hold the key.

Stricter laws prevent some things, but they can't change the hearts of those who wield weapons.

Jesus Christ, The One in you, He can.[7] Follow His Voice and step out to fight for your streets.

When Nehemiah worked to rebuild the wall, he knew enemies marched on the city, but the wall was unfinished. Instead of placing the most experienced fighters to defend the weak places in the walls, he hand-selected fathers and husbands.[8] He knew when a man defends his family he is the fiercest opponent.

These are our families. God handpicked you. Get up and fight!

No more debating on social media. No more helpless head shaking while watching the news.

You want to converse on social media?

Great, record or write a prayer with Scripture and post it. "For the word of God is quick, and powerful, and sharper than any two-edged sword, piercing even to the dividing asunder of soul and spirit, and of the joints and marrow, and is a discerner of the thoughts and intents of the heart."[9]

Use Scriptures in the comment section rather than arguments. No matter how well-worded, debates fall on deaf ears of angry people.

You want to watch the news. Great, but then shut it off and walk the streets of your neighborhood, pleading the blood of The Lamb over every single door.10

Aren't you over this?

I'm tired of it. I'm not lamenting anymore. I'm furious.

No more. No more of this in our schools or our communities.

We need to come out of slumber and unite. Baptists, Lutherans, Catholics — no matter what it says on your church sign. If you believe Jesus is the One and only way, truth, and life,11 get out your war drum and join brothers and sisters on the street.

Let's go. Will you march out with me? On the 19th of September from each year I will be walking around the schools closest to me and claiming the land in the name of Jesus. Will you be there?

Let's get our instruments like David when he moved the ark and worshiped God during the journey.12 We march on our enemy with a megaphone declaring this land as God's, affirming the precious Blood of Jesus over our streets and businesses.

Come with me.

We are Joshua and his army marching around the city of Jericho until God tells us to shout.13 When He gives the order, shout with me the battle cry of your heart.

142

Shout for the parents whose children were taken, for your marriages, your neighbors and your babies. Shout for the racial separation and the plague of lust upon our people. The time for rest ends. The fog of winter lifted, and spring comes.

Let's praise the name of Jesus in our streets and shout down the walls of the enemy. These are our people, this is our land.

Enough is enough.

Day 38. May I See With Your Eyes.

There is a young woman smoking a cigarette on break outside the grocery store. *Within her I see a black ball of yarn. Someone unravels it and rolls it back together into a messy tangled mass.*

He moves me to speak. I lean against the wall out of her sight. Are you sure? What do you want me to say?

Go to her. Kneel before her and pray at her feet.

Is she having issues with her feet?

Go to her. Kneel before her and pray at her feet.

The Holy Spirit does not always elaborate on the meaning of my visions. If I interpret them apart from Him they are spoiled by my personal worldview, bias, and cultural context. I can't allow my perspective to influence these visions, which are representations of an individual's life story.

Waiting, I close my eyes and drop my head against the rock wall, feeling the light of the afternoon sun warm my cheeks. *What is the tangle, Lord?* Waiting. *What is the yarn?*

Silence.

The entangled woman's co-worker approaches. They engage in idle chatter about the long shift ahead. I decide no more information will arrive from the Lord and retrieve my cart. *When I finish shopping, if she is still there, then I will pray.* Before I separate the cart from its stack, the conversation ends. No more excuses.

"Hey, can I sit here?" I approach, no longer as afraid or awkward. Okay, maybe still a bit awkward.

She nods, smiling around the cigarette in her mouth, turns her head and releases the smoke away from me. "Of course."

"This may sound strange," I say, "but I believe in Jesus Christ. He shows me things about people. When I looked at you, I saw a messy tangle of black yarn in your heart. It appeared as an unraveled coil put back together poorly. I wondered if I could pray over you about what I saw?"

She is intrigued, "Yes, that would be great!"

Kneel before her and pray at her feet.

I draw myself to my knees on the sidewalk, placing my hands on her black shoes. She straightens and tries to move the cigarette away.

"Don't worry about that, it doesn't bother me. I know you're on your break."

"Thank you." She murmurs.

Unsure of what to pray, my clipped words reach and strain. "Thank you, God for Your great love for this precious woman. I declare freedom over her life from anything entangling or trapping her. I bless her with the unraveling of Your truth. May You reveal it. In the name of Jesus, amen."

"I needed that. Thank you. I'm Callie," She extinguishes her finished cigarette and we shake hands. "A child was just stillborn in my family a few days ago. It is a tragic week for us."

Grief twists my stomach. "I am so sorry."

"My nephew's child. A full-term boy, at 39 weeks. Their first baby."
I see the first moment I held my new son in my arms, the rejoicing of our family in those days, tears blur my vision. *What loss this family suffered.* "I am so sorry." I repeat.

"I'm here, you know. I'm working." Callie confides, "but I am not really here. Kind of a shell." She forces her eyes to blink. "What you have is a gift. Most people would not appreciate it, but I do. I have a gift too, well, it's more like a curse. I am empathic. It takes over my life because I receive negative emotions from others and I don't know how to let them go. I carry it all inside until I can't function."

"Maybe the Lord is showing me a myriad of emotions all tangled up in you. God gave you this gift not to burden you," I say, "But so you can show love to others and pray for them effectively. Jesus said, 'Come to me, all you who are weary and burdened, and I will give you rest.[14] He says to 'cast all our anxiety on Him because He cares for you'."[15]

Callie nods. "It would be nice to learn how to control this rather than have it controlling me."

I tell her that I will keep her nephew and his wife in my prayers. "The Lord says, 'My joy comes in the morning'. I will pray for their morning to come swiftly."

Callie never said she was a Christian, I suspect she was being polite in not disagreeing with me about who the Lord is, and where these gifts come from.

Maybe when I grow up a little more in this gift, I will discern such things in the moment.

Maybe what I said was all Callie needed to hear right now.

Maybe I just need to stop questioning everything and keep my eyes fixed on Jesus.[16]

Maybe. Maybe. Maybe.

Day 40. The End of a Season.

Gwen and I meet once a week now to fellowship and pray *together.*

The Holy Spirit reminded her that she is called to pray for men. I once promised to take up Gwen's torch if she died. What a relief she lives because I don't possess the gifting for this global prayer.

"I pray for every man in every house," she speaks beautifully and empowering. "On every street. In every city. In every state and region. In every country. On every continent. I pray for every baby boy, every child, every man young and old. May courage rise in you. Care for your families and provide for your homes with honorable hard work. Be cared for with tenderness and respected by the women in your lives. Love and cherish them more than yourself. I pray your trials strengthen rather than damage, and that the example of Jesus Christ shape you, body, heart, and spirit. Father God protect our boys. Protect our baby boys from the corruption of this world. May they know You intimately. God bless every man in every house…"

"In the name of Jesus, for His Glory and by the power of His blood, Amen." I say in agreement.

Gwen likes her new clinic. Dialysis is not the torture chamber it once was. She admits at least three people should lose their jobs at the other treatment center. She decided not to speak against them publicly, however, for fear of losing good standing with her current clinic.

I pray God will intervene with swift justice there. If anyone suffers like Gwen, may they be filled with hope and treated with love, and no one else be driven to the deadly decision Gwen was forced to make.

Gwen and I are not the only ones who made dramatic changes lately. Baby Leroy is not much of a baby anymore. He toddles around the house wreaking havoc on the dogs and figuring out how to climb everything. How wonderful to see him grow strong. Is that how the Father feels when watching my own explorations?

A wave of Jesus' love washes over me, and I know I am more spirit than flesh because I cannot physically contain the encounter. The world I see through His filter is one of light, joy, and fullness of life. He owes me nothing and yet He gave me everything.

Forty days have passed since the day Gwen and I prayed for her life. In the Bible, 40 days symbolizes periods of trial and testing that close in victory and discipline.

Today marks the end of a season, and the beginning of something new.

Part VIII Scriptures

1) Look up Nehemiah 4:1-15

2) 2 Timothy 4:7 I have fought a good fight, I have finished my course, I have kept the faith.

3) Psalm 103:5 Who satisfieth thy mouth with good things; so that thy youth is renewed like the eagle's.

4) Psalm 34:8 O taste and see that the Lord is good: blessed is the man that trusteth in him.

5) Isaiah 40:3-5 The voice of him that crieth in the wilderness, Prepare ye the way of the Lord, make straight in the desert a highway for our God. Every valley shall be exalted, and every mountain and hill shall be made low: and the crooked shall be made straight, and the rough places plain: And the glory of the Lord shall be revealed, and all flesh shall see it together: for the mouth of the Lord hath spoken it.

6) 1 Corinthians 3:1-2 And I, brethren, could not speak unto you as unto spiritual, but as unto carnal, even as unto babes in Christ. I have fed you with milk, and not with meat: for hitherto ye were not able to bear it, neither yet now are ye able.

7) 1 John 4:4 Ye are of God, little children, and have overcome them: because greater is he that is in you, than he that is in the world.

8) Nehemiah 4:13-14 Therefore set I in the lower places behind the wall, and on the higher places, I even set the people after their families with their swords, their spears, and their bows. And I looked,

and rose up, and said unto the nobles, and to the rulers, and to the rest of the people, Be not ye afraid of them: remember the Lord, which is great and terrible, and fight for your brethren, your sons, and your daughters, your wives, and your houses.

9) Hebrews 4:12 For the word of God is quick, and powerful, and sharper than any two-edged sword, piercing even to the dividing asunder of soul and spirit, and of the joints and marrow, and is a discerner of the thoughts and intents of the heart.

10) Exodus 4:5-7,13 Your lamb shall be without blemish, a male of the first year: ye shall take it out from the sheep, or from the goats: And ye shall keep it up until the fourteenth day of the same month: and the whole assembly of the congregation of Israel shall kill it in the evening. And they shall take of the blood, and strike it on the two side posts and on the upper door post of the houses, wherein they shall eat it... And the blood shall be to you for a token upon the houses where ye are: and when I see the blood, I will pass over you, and the plague shall not be upon you to destroy you, when I smite the land of Egypt.

11) John 14:6 Jesus saith unto him, I am the way, the truth, and the life: no man cometh unto the Father, but by me.

12) 2 Samuel 6:15 So David and all the house of Israel brought up the ark of the Lord with shouting, and with the sound of the trumpet.

13) Joshua 6: 20 So the people shouted when the priests blew with the trumpets: and it came to pass, when the people heard the sound of the trumpet, and the people shouted with a great shout, that the wall fell down flat, so that the people went up into the city, every man straight before him, and they took the city.

14) Matthew 11:28-30 Come to me, all who labor and are heavy laden, and I will give you rest. Take my yoke upon you, and learn from me, for I am gentle and lowly in heart, and you will find rest for your souls. For my yoke is easy, and my burden is light.

15) 1 Peter 5:7 Casting all your care upon him; for he careth for you.

16) Hebrews 12:2 Looking unto Jesus the author and finisher of our faith; who for the joy that was set before him endured the cross, despising the shame, and is set down at the right hand of the throne of God.

Part IX:

Home

I stroll Leroy along on this glorious last Saturday in April.

Flowers are bursting open and the smell of lilac reigns over my neighborhood. Gwen's house comes into view through the blossoming trees.

She attempts to mow her front yard. It's hard work, only a few rows are complete and already she empties the bag, moving as if bricks are shackled to her ankles. This chore will take her all day. Some of her strength has returned, thanks to consistent dialysis, but excess fluid remains in her lungs and heart. It strains her body and depletes her energy.

Like our first encounter eleven months ago, I arrive on time for a divine appointment, pushing my toe-headed child and waving. Unlike that first meeting, today we greet as family. "Hey there, sister." I call, surveying her long grass and the sloping earth of the lawn. She melts into her wicker backless seat gasping for air and smiling as bright as the morning sunlight.

"What's up, sis? Hi Leroy, do you see all these beautiful flowers?"

Wanting to get to her, he tries to undo the straps imprisoning him in the stroller. "How about you hang out with this cute kid and I mow the rest for you." The words seem like an offer, but I have an assignment from the Lord.

"Yes!" She takes the lead of the stroller and I grab the mower. The rise and fall of the earth, and my lack of motor skills, make for a difficult lawn to mow. But I love my beautiful audience. At each turn I see Leroy and Gwen engaged in joyful chatter watching me from her porch. He sits on her lap, encircled in her arms, their cheeks touching. Leroy's dimples deepen, his wide smile mirroring Gwen's as they point at me. Waving and clapping, they cheer me on like I am the prized float in a mowing parade. I make quicker, wobblier work of the backyard.

Gwen and I laugh when we survey my drunken lines. She holds Leroy on her hip, rocking him in a loving hug. "Praise God you came. Today is my grandson's 6th birthday. I almost spent my energy on this stupid chore when I needed to save it for his party later."

"No worries, I loved doing it. Are you okay with Leroy? I want to go downstairs and see the progress." Gwen waves me in, staying outside to play with Leroy amidst the smell of fresh cut grass. I head to the basement. Ethan has been working hard on the remodel for weeks. Gwen expects his family to move in by the end of May.

Gwen has shared with me a conversation she had with her grandson a few weeks back. They were together in the living room, Ethan working downstairs. "Do you know what dad is doing?" he asked.

"Something pretty cool. What do you think he's doing?" Gwen tested. Her grandson looked out the window to the street, giddy with quiet excitement.

"He builds us a home." He told her, his small chest swollen with pride.

God has provided for the project in creative ways. Ethan finds quality used items for prices that only make sense when you give God the credit, His faithfulness shining through every wall, light, and bit of flooring.

Joyful tears blur my vision as I view the home taking shape. Framing is up in a place once exposed by cold concrete and piping. I imagine the finished product: the living room with cherry hard wood flooring bought for a mere $100 from a couple who decided they wanted a new color. A kitchenette there, with left-over tile found in my garage. And a spacious bathroom with the granite sink and a soak tub Ethan discovered at a thrift store. Gwen can't wait for that soak tub, "It's big enough for a pool party!" she marveled.

This is a place designed to make memories. God quieted both of Gwen's fears, no longer will she have to struggle to make payments for the house, and she can provide an affordable space for Ethan's family.

"You look great, Gwen." I say when I return to strap Leroy in his stroller.

"Thanks! The doctors expect the fluid in my lungs to recede over time. But they can't figure out why my heart is enlarged right now."

157

Fear sinks to the pit of my stomach. "That doesn't sound good."

"They say it will also go down eventually. Don't be worried; they weren't." Back on dialysis for three months now, Gwen continues to like her new clinic. She seizes any opportunity to share the hope of Jesus with the patients and staff. "I keep getting comments on my skin," she says. "A few other patients told me I glow. People ask all the time what I do for my skin to make it look that way."

"Moses!" We say at the same time and giggle.

"Yep," Gwen continues, "Like when Moses returned from the mountain top aglow because he witnessed the glory of God. No fancy creams, I promise. I don't need 'em; I saw His glory! We are all stuck to the machines, so the other patients can't escape as I talk about Jesus for those next hours."

Leroy starts grumpy wiggling. "My toddler timer is up. I better head home. Have so much fun at the party." We give her a group hug.

"Oh, I will. Can I cook you a fancy dinner next week? I want to get you back for my awesome mowed lawn."

"That would be great! Good thing you cook better than I mow."

"It will be my best meal yet," Gwen promises. "Sometime in the next week, not sure which day. We will work it out. I can't thank you enough; you have no idea how much this meant to me."

The walk home is full of bird songs, my step light and joyful.

Day 116. The Sunset.

I spoke to Gwen on the phone the next Saturday.

We talk for an hour about the blessing of her grandson's party. "I would have been a lump in the chair if you never came by and mowed. That was totally God's timing! You should have seen my sweet big six-year-old; we enjoyed a perfect day."

She had already started prepping for my special dinner and planned to bring it the next night. "I am making lemon-crusted salmon with a side of slow roasted parmesan cauliflower. I'm thinking of dipping the salmon in a parmesan mix too, so the whole thing has a nice cheesy flavor. The way you like it. I plan to start defrosting the fish in the morning, so let me know what your day looks like tomorrow afternoon. I want it on your table hot." We agree on 5 o'clock for her to bring my feast. She won't stay, Leroy fights a cold and neither of us want her to catch it.

I watched a movie with Leroy on Sunday evening. The light of late afternoon began to fade, and my stomach growled, I checked the clock on my phone. Where's Gwen, it's 5? I realized I forgot to send her a message in the morning like she asked. I texted her at 5:13 pm but received no response. I checked my phone often, arguing with my worries.

This isn't the first time I haven't heard back from her. If she didn't answer on purpose, if she feels too crummy to cook, I don't want her to feel bad.

It is weird she wouldn't answer about something like this. She promised me. It's unlike her to break a promise. She said she needed to get her cauliflower cooked today.

Maybe she forgot. Maybe she spent the day with Ethan and it slipped her mind. I'll check back tomorrow, and we'll laugh about it.

Now it's Monday. I sent another message but never heard anything.

I drive by Gwen's house on the way to get groceries. It is dark inside, her car in the driveway. I check the clock as I pass. 10:38 a.m. She should be at dialysis right now. I reach for my phone thinking maybe I should call and check on her. Even though her car is there, it feels like no one is home. Dark, no lights or television on, which they usually are.

What a snoopy neighbor I am, to know such things. She probably ended up having a rough weekend after we spoke on Saturday and went to Ethan's house. I bet he took her to dialysis.

Today is a good day because Tylor returns from a long business trip. After the grocery store, Leroy and I shake with excitement, driving to retrieve him. When I pull into the airport parking lot I look to the sky and gasp. Months ago, when I was a different person and this adventure first began, a vision of clouds and light came upon me. Fluffy textures of white, grey, and sunlight. Just like the sky, at this exact moment.

My son gets impatient as I take time to snap pictures, and gaze at the beauty of the sun starting to set. "Okay, okay, Bubbies. Let's go get Da. I know, I miss him too!"

Later my reunited family pulls onto our street. I steal a glance at Gwen's house as we pass. *Good. Ethan's truck is there now.* I sigh with relief and settle back in the car. *Everything is fine. Right? I will call Gwen tomorrow and make new dinner plans. I'm hoping…well, yea. Everything must be fine.*

Day 117. System Error.

I worry for Gwen all day.

I noticed Ethan's truck again when I drive by. He is out talking with a neighbor. They stand in the middle of the street and don't move much to make way for my car.

That's weird.

I wave, and Ethan looks right through me.

He doesn't recognize me. I decide. My hand dropping at the expression on his face. My stomach forms a sticky web.

I reach for the phone several times after that, wanting to call her. *I wonder if she is in the hospital. Would Ethan think to tell me?*

The vision of the sky returns, I see the sunset filled with bright clouds. The picture I took yesterday. Holy Spirit layers another image on top. The silhouette of a fisherman, casting out a net.

The sticky web expands. I pick up my phone and stare at the screen.

I don't want to know. If she is gone. I don't want to know yet. I set the phone aside face down. *Everything is probably fine.*

When it rings a few hours later, my heart leaps into my throat, gasping with relief. *Gwen! It's Gwen calling!* I answer before it rings a second time.

"Gwen! Hey sister, I've been worried about you!"

"Erinn." It's Ethan.

No more pretending.

You knew it wasn't fine, didn't you?

I did too. I knew.

"Ethan. Is everything okay?"

"No. It's not, Erinn. I hate calling to tell you this. I wanted to come by and..." I wait for him to gather his thoughts. "Mom is gone. She passed away yesterday. They think late morning. Mid-afternoon, or something."

"What happened? We just spoke on Saturday, she sounded fine. She even mowed her lawn."

She said it was easier because my mow made for shorter grass. She promised me my special dinner.

Now? How is she gone now? After everything that happened? Grief is like a faulty technology update. Lose someone you love and there is a lot of failed downloads.

Please wait...system download may take 934 minutes...

She looked forward to Leroy's second birthday next month. They love each other. They are such dear friends. No. They were. How did Gwen go from the present to a person of my past?

Download Unsecure. Do you want to continue?...

She thought of getting him a tool belt for his present. I never got a picture of them together. I never got a picture of us together. I don't have any pictures of Gwen at all.

"I found her yesterday after the dialysis center called to tell me she never came for her appointment." Ethan's voice cuts through my racing thoughts. "Her legs were crossed at the ankles and her arms folded in her lap on the bathroom floor. I said good bye while waiting for the coroner and police to arrive.

"I wandered around the house, figuring out her last hours," he explained. "Seems like she felt unwell in the bathroom. I can tell that she got up to get a glass of water and her phone. Then she got comfortable again on the bathroom floor. I bet she figured she would call for us after she rested. She looked peaceful, comfortable, where I found her."

My own voice echoes across time, *Gwen, in the name of Jesus, I declare you will not die of suffocation. When your appointed time comes, you enter His Kingdom with a spirit of peace not fear. You will not suffer. You will fall into a sweet sleep and awaken to the face of Jesus! 'Do not be afraid, for I am with you,' says the Lord! Only peace and rejoicing for you in these last days! In the name of Jesus and by the power of His blood, amen!*

165

I bite my wrist, so Ethan will not hear my tear-filled gasping. I try to listen as he continues. He tells me she loved me. How grateful he is for the time we spent together. "Most friends disappear when times are hardest. Not you. You came around when things got bad."

How can I explain what a blessing it was to call her friend and all I did for her returned to me tenfold?

Gwen is on my couch with her arms around Leroy. "Your birthday is coming." She plants a solid kiss on his temple and sets his squirming figure free, "What should I get you. You deserve the best gift."

Downloading...

"I wanted to tell you in person, but things got crazy yesterday and I couldn't make it over there." Ethan continues, "I didn't want you to be in the dark any longer and, I don't know. I don't think I could have said this to you face-to-face anyway. I will never forget what you did for my mother."

How could he know it was not me but the Lord I serve who accomplished these things?

I remember Gwen's voice, like smooth music, her melody cracking with passionate tears. "I pray for every man in every house. On every street. In every city..."

I pace a pathway in my backyard as I listen. Back and forth. Neurotic swift steps along the fence line. Painful tears forcing streams down my cheeks. My husband comes out and Leroy runs toward me with arms outstretched. I can't face them yet. For the first time in his life, I turn my back on Leroy when he asks for me and continue my pacing.

Back and forth.

In my mind I hear her sweet voice, how she would roll her R's and get quieter when she was excited about something. *"I've worked on these cherry tarts all day. I don't mean to brag, but they are the best thing I have ever eaten. Can I drop some by? You have to promise to share with Leroy!"*

"Mom is where she wants to be. Where she wanted to be all along." Ethan says. He tells me about his son's party, how thankful he is for those memories and the pictures of his child with his mother from that day. "I would not have this picture, if she didn't decide to live a little longer."

I remember Gwen wrapped in Leroy's dragon blanket. *Shivering, she pulls it high on her shoulders. "You know what I think about all the time? It is this tiny moment from my life, maybe lasted 20 minutes. But every time I remember, it warms me up. My grandson was Leroy's age, just a baby starting to talk. I watched him one night, and as we waited for his parents to come home it began to rain. I turned all the lights off, snuggled tight in a blanket and we sat by the window. 'Listen.' I whispered, 'That is rain. Doesn't it sound beautiful?' He looked so full of wonder, and he curled into me. We listened to the rain together, whispering to each other. How strange. These moments we hold dearest at the end of our lives they are sometimes the simplest."*

Downloading...

"I don't know if this is bad or what, but I haven't cried yet." Ethan says, sounding confused.

I don't have an answer for him. I'm confused too.

System Error. Download failed... Retry?

Day 139. The Final Cast.

Father? I'm so confused. I need you.

His Spirit speaks.

I will go before you and make the crooked places straight, He says. **I will break in pieces the gates of brass and cut in sunder the bars of iron.**

Peering through the film of greasy child fingerprints and dog-nose smudges out my bay window to the street, I remember a time just over 12 months ago.

I see me, a different me, struggling to turn the secondhand stroller from my driveway onto the cracked sidewalk. Leroy, a baby not yet one year, gazes up at me with joy, his fluffy blonde hair ruffles like soft feathers in the morning sunlight.

This is it! It is about to begin! I want to wave and call to myself. *You have no idea what you are about to walk into. . .*

That morning I met a woman who changed my life. God lead us on a journey, revealed the power of His mighty love, then He called her home, where she wanted to be.

Leroy looks for her. When we walk past her house I have to hold him back from running up to the door. It is Ethan's house now, he keeps to himself in his grief. "She is not there anymore, sweetie." I tell my darling

169

boy. "Gwen lives in Jesus' house now. We will see her again someday." He nods with a knowing look in serious blue eyes and moves on.

I grasp for the same level of acceptance.

What happens now? I cannot return to the person I once was. Lord?

Come. He says, calling me to meet with Him in a special place within my spirit.

Would you come with us? I want you to seek solace there too.

Close your eyes and silence the noise. Clear the space until all that remains is grey nothingness. Now a stone wall appears before us, reaching up, up, out of sight into the grey void above. I place my hand on the stone and am drawn inside a lush, wild garden. The King of Heaven tends this place for me when I am away.

Refreshing moisture hangs in the air. Straight ahead is a path of soft grass weaving through a variety of lush plants that opens into a clearing. Before me a pool shimmers at the base of mature trees. A willow, an oak, and an evergreen stretch over it. The quiet pool reflects their splendor.

I planted those trees many years ago to symbolize my family. My husband, Leroy, and the second child I pray to have one day. When I pray for them, Jesus and I lay hands on their trunks. To the left is a wild rose bush I pray over for healing for my mom. And I put those jalapeno plants there for my dad.

Next to these is my favorite spot in all the universes. A stone bench, large enough for two, looks upon a river. Sometimes the river runs fast with white water. Other seasons it is slower, warm, pleasant to swim in. It is filled with fish, if you quiet yourself they swim up to you.

Standing beside this bench, my Lord waits for us. Clothed in light and on His head a crown like stars. He dims it for me on mornings like this, knowing I need to see His face.

Jesus. The Creator of the heavens and the earth here to comfort me. Why is He smiling? He knows my broken heart.

He beckons me to sit beside Him on the bank of the river. He puts His bare feet in the water and I watch the current gliding over His toes. It reflects His soft light.

What now, Lord? How does this all end? I say. Unable to hide my defeat, I dip my fingers in the water and pull them out to watch drops fall. Warmer than I expected.

It doesn't end. He glances at me then wiggles His submerged toes to make me giggle.

I don't know why, but it works.

Why do this? Why me? I gaze into His glorious face.

Because you are strong enough. I know you. I know what you can handle and what you are good at. I know what you are capable of. You could have said 'no', but you agreed.

He wiggles His toes again, drawing a curious fish close before it dashes into deeper waters.

And why would Gwen die after she decided to live?

It was her appointed time. She chose life. She chose to let Me take her home on My terms. Some things are between Gwen and Me.

I don't get it. This isn't what I thought would happen. She was doing so well. What was the point to everything we went through?

Choose life.

Choose life and then die. I shouldn't be sarcastic with the Almighty Creator. I should be reverent.

Instead of chastising me, He answers through opening my eyes to a vision:

Gwen is running a marathon. One final hill needs climbing. Downhill on the other side is the finish line. She only sees the hill, not realizing how close she is. She slows, then stops at its base. She grips her knees, takes heaving breaths. Her gasps turn to sobs from the pain and exhaustion of her race. She collapses.

Then here I come. I jog up to her with a paper cup of water, rub her shoulders, and say something that must be funny because it makes her smile. I step back and start clapping and cheering.

172

"Get up! Get going! Your almost there! Go, go, go!" I jump and cheer.

Leroy is there too, clapping his baby hands and laughing. We do a silly dance as we cheer her name. She smiles faintly but will not move. Leroy steps forward and kisses Gwen's cheek, holding her face gently. "It is time to get up." I say and reach a hand out.

She looks at it for moment then a smile spreads and she takes it. She finishes the water. My arm goes around her waist, she slings one of hers over my shoulder and holds Leroy's hand with her free one. We climb the hill together. At the top, Gwen looks back to see how far she came. Her face begins to glow. She squeezes Leroy's hand then lets go.

She is running.

Down the hill and laughing, toward the finish line, her arms outstretched like she will lift off into flight. Leroy and I watch from the hilltop, cheering as our friend barrels toward the celebrating crowd on the other side of the finish line.

She makes it. Before crossing, she turns to blow us one last kiss and disappears into light.

Home.

I raise my head. We are still in the prayer garden. The Lord's face shines like sunshine reflected in water, His eyes soft and His smile filled with love. **You did what I asked of you. You did well, my child.**

This time the tears welling up soothe rather than ache. *What now, Jesus?*

173

He cups a hand in the running water and draws some out. It shimmers in His palm like wet paint. He dips a thumb inside and begins to wash my face. I feel His touch on my cheeks as He wipes the tears away.

My grief no longer cripples, it fortifies.

Jesus raises His hand above my head and releases the rest of the water over me. I close my eyes and feel it flow down my face, my hair, my back. He places His hands on each of my cheeks and we lean forward until my forehead rests on His.

Breathe in deep, renewed.

Now, He says, ***you cast the net out one more time.***

Epilogue. A Love So Mighty.

Before Gwen passed on into Glory, even before she decided to live, there was a morning the Lord called me to continue recording the events transpiring around me...

"Day 14", I type and stare at my screen. *What crazy things do You have for me today?*

"I am worried." I enter and then delete it. "How will this end?" I type instead then bow my head and pray.

Will Gwen die or be healed? When will I know this story is finished? Can an eternal story ever finish? I ask.

Love. It is about My Love.

Love? What do you mean?

Finish it right now. Finish it with Love.

I am still halfway through this adventure. How strange to write the ending now when it just began. But for you, this testimony has a few pages left.

He opens my eyes and I see the sky at sunset. Clouds and light. Fluffy textures of white, grey, and sun.

The vision changes to someone curled on a couch reading these words. Rain comes down in glistening

175

rivers on the window at their right. They wear blue pants and a light-colored sweater.

I see...

A man at night with a cup of coffee in a dim room, one light on. He takes a break from reading to check the clock.

A book at its end. The final pages curling in hands ready for the work of God.

A speed reader rapidly swiping the screen of their tablet. A cracked screen like mine. Did your toddler drop yours too?

You. I see you with your guitar in a messy room. Pick it up right now and start strumming. The chords are locked away in your heart, He prepares to unleash them.

Multitudes reading, hearing, receiving a testimony of God's love.

I am overcome by the Everlasting Love He has for you. Can you feel it coming through? Take a second to receive.

A mighty and majestic encounter washes over you. The force of His love disintegrates your grief, chains, your facades. He stirs through time and words to get to your heart.

This part of my story ends. The next part is yours to tell, write, sing, and whisper to your children.

In the story of Jesus Christ, God the Father, and the Holy Spirit sent to us, stories of the disciples, the mother sitting up with her sick child, the couple persevering through a difficult marriage. All our stories have the same thing in common...Without love it is meaningless.

Our Lord is Love. All love moves from Him and through Him. Try and work anything apart from His Love and when you make mistakes you destroy. But with love, well, He says, **love covers a multitude of sins**.

Open your heart so He may use you as a vessel to pour His Mighty Love out into the hands of the thirsty. Be renewed by an eternal joy. Even if what He asks makes no sense, seems weird, makes you look crazy. Don't miss the chance to be part of a miracle.

Offer water. Don't you see? Everyone is thirsty. Everyone. God readies to open the wells in each of you. Wells of Living Water.

Please, *please*, don't put this book down and think, "Aww, what a nice story." Then go about your lives like you are a normal person.

No! You are not a normal person!

You are a wellspring in the desert. A light in darkness, a City on a Hill where weary travelers seek shelter.

You are a warrior.

You are called forward. Do you think you made it to these last pages, if it were not so? Stop messing around. People are dying of thirst out there.

Open your heart and allow His love in today. It will transform you, exploding in your life and detonating the lives around you with uncontainable love.

That is how this story ends and yours begins. End with His Love. Begin with His Love.

I cannot wait to pick up the story you write.

With Abounding Love and Joy in Jesus Christ,

Erinn Josephine Campton

About the Author

Erinn has walked with Jesus her entire life and has been writing for nearly that long. Her best days are spent in a cuddle pile with a little boy and three semi-naughty canines while her soulmate is nearby tinkering in his garage.

Born and raised in Northern Colorado, she is closest to our Lord when sitting on a mountain beside a river with a cup of coffee in one hand and a book in the other.

She currently has ceased her career as a telemarketer to start Chain Breaker Limited, a business that creates marketing content and support for small businesses.

She invites you to reach out to her with prayer requests, praise reports, and small business ownership frustrations. You are welcome to connect with her online through her website or social media (Facebook, Instagram, Twitter).

www.erinnjcampton.com
@erinnjcampton

Made in the USA
Monee, IL
16 September 2019